SHEPHERD'S NOTES

Shepherd's Notes Titles Available

SHEPHERD'S NOTES COMMENTARY SERIES

Old Testament

9-780-805-490-282 Genesis
9-780-805-490-565 Exodus
9-780-805-490-695 Leviticus, Numbers
9-780-805-490-275 Deuteronomy
9-780-805-490-589 Joshua, Judges
9-780-805-490-572 Ruth, Esther
9-780-805-490-633 1 & 2 Samuel
9-780-805-490-077 1 & 2 Kings
9-780-805-490-649 1 & 2 Chronicles
9-780-805-491-944 Ezra, Nehemiah
9-780-805-490-060 Job
9-780-805-493-399 Psalms 1-50

9-780-805-493-405 Psalms 51-100
9-780-805-493-412 Psalms 101-150
9-780-805-490-169 Proverbs
9-780-805-490-596 Ecclesiastes, Song of Solomon
9-780-805-491-975 Isaiah
9-780-805-490-701 Jeremiah, Lamentations
9-780-805-490-787 Ezekiel
9-780-805-490-152 Daniel
9-780-805-493-269 Hosea, Obadiah
9-780-805-493-344 Jonah, Zephaniah
9-780-805-490-657 Haggai, Malachi

New Testament

9-781-558-196-889 Matthew
9-780-805-490-718 Mark
9-780-805-490-046 Luke
9-781-558-196-933 John
9-781-558-196-919 Acts
9-780-805-490-053 Romans
9-780-805-493-252 1 Corinthians
9-780-805-493-351 2 Corinthians
9-781-558-196-902 Galatians
9-780-805-493-276 Ephesians

9-781-558-196-896 Philippians, Colossians, Philemon
9-780-805-490-008 1 & 2 Thessalonians
9-781-558-196-926 1 & 2 Timothy, Titus
9-780-805-493-368 Hebrews
9-780-805-490-183 James
9-780-805-490-190 1 & 2 Peter & Jude
9-780-805-492-149 1, 2 & 3 John
9-780-805-490-176 Revelation

SHEPHERD'S NOTES CHRISTIAN CLASSICS

9-780-805-493-474 *Mere Christianity,* C. S. Lewis
9-780-805-493-535 *The Problem of Pain/ A Grief Observed,* C. S. Lewis
9-780-805-491-999 *The Confessions,* Augustine
9-780-805-492-002 *Calvin's Institutes*
9-780-805-493-948 *Miracles,* C. S. Lewis

9-780-805-491-968 *Lectures to My Students,* Charles Haddon Spurgeon
9-780-805-492-200 *The Writings of Justin Martyr*
9-780-805-493-450 *The City of God,* Augustine
9-780-805-491-982 *The Cost of Discipleship,* Bonhoeffer

SHEPHERD'S NOTES — BIBLE SUMMARY SERIES

9-780-805-493-771 Old Testament
9-780-805-493-788 New Testament

9-780-805-493-849 Life & Teachings of Jesus
9-780-805-493-856 Life & Letters of Paul

SHEPHERD'S NOTES

When you need a guide through the Scriptures

Psalms 1-50

HOLMAN
REFERENCE

NASHVILLE, TENNESSEE

Shepherd's Notes®—*Psalms 1–50*
© 1999
by B&H Publishing Group
Nashville, Tennessee
All rights reserved
Printed in the United States of America

978-0-8054-9339-9
Dewey Decimal Classification: 223.20
Subject Heading: BIBLE. O.T. PSALMS
Library of Congress Card Catalog Number: 98–48095

Library of Congress Cataloging-in-Publication Data
Gould, Dana, 1951–
Psalms 1–50 / Dana Gould, editor [i.e. author].
    p.   cm. — (Shepherd's notes)
Includes bibliographical references.
ISBN 0-8054-9339-5
    1. Bible. O.T. Psalms—Study and teaching. I. Title. II. Title: Psalms
one–fifty. III. Series
  BS1430.5.G68 1999
  223'.207—dc21

                                              98–48095
                                               CIP

7 8 9 10 11 12   16 15 14 13 12

CONTENTS

FOREWORD

Dear Reader:

Shepherd's Notes are designed to give you a quick, step-by-step overview of every book of the Bible. They are not meant to be substitutes for the biblical text; rather, they are study guides intended to help you explore the wisdom of Scripture in personal or group study and to apply that wisdom successfully in your own life.

Shepherd's Notes guide you through the main themes of each book of the Bible and illuminate fascinating details through appropriate commentary and reference notes. Historical and cultural background information brings the Bible into sharper focus.

Six different icons, used throughout the series, call your attention to historical-cultural information, Old Testament and New Testament references, word pictures, unit summaries, and personal application for everyday life.

Whether you are a novice or a veteran at Bible study, I believe you will find *Shepherd's Notes* a resource that will take you to a new level in your mining and applying the riches of Scripture.

In Him,

David R. Shepherd
Editor-in-Chief

DESIGNED FOR THE BUSY USER

Shepherd's Notes for Psalms 1–50 is designed to provide an easy-to-use tool for getting a quick handle on this portion of this significant Bible book's important features, and for gaining an understanding of their messages. Information available in more difficult-to-use reference works has been incorporated into the *Shepherd's Notes* format. This brings you the benefits of many advanced and expensive works packed into one small volume.

Shepherd's Notes are for laymen, pastors, teachers, small-group leaders and participants, as well as the classroom student. Enrich your personal study or quiet time. Shorten your class or small-group preparation time as you gain valuable insights into the truths of God's Word that you can pass along to your students or group members.

DESIGNED FOR QUICK ACCESS

Bible students with time constraints will especially appreciate the timesaving features built into the *Shepherd's Notes*. All features are intended to aid a quick and concise encounter with the heart of the messages of Psalms 1–50.

Concise Commentary. Short sections provide quick "snapshots" of the themes of the psalms.

Outlined Text. Comprehensive outlines cover the entire text of Psalms 1–50. This is a valuable feature for following each book's flow, allowing for a quick, easy way to locate a particular passage.

Shepherd's Notes. These summary statements or capsule thoughts appear at the close of every key section of the narratives. While functioning in part as a quick summary, they also deliver the essence of the message presented in the sections which they cover.

Icons. Various icons in the margin highlight recurring themes in Psalms 1–50, aiding in selective searching or tracing of those themes.

Questions to Guide Your Study. These thought-provoking questions and discussion starters are designed to encourage interaction with the truth and principles of God's Word.

DESIGNED TO WORK FOR YOU

Personal Study. Using the *Shepherd's Notes* with a passage of Scripture can enlighten your study and take it to a new level. At your fingertips is information that would require searching several volumes to find. In addition, many points of application occur throughout the volume, contributing to personal growth.

Teaching. Outlines frame the text of Psalms 1–50, providing a logical presentation of their messages. Capsule thoughts designated as "Shepherd's Notes" provide summary statements for presenting the essence of key points and events. Application icons point out personal application of the messages of the books. Historical Context icons indicate where cultural and historical background information is supplied.

Group Study. *Shepherd's Notes* can be an excellent companion volume to use for gaining a quick but accurate understanding of the messages of Psalms 1–50. Each group member can benefit from having his or her own copy. The *Note's* format accommodates the study of themes throughout Psalms 1–50. Leaders may use its flexible features to prepare for group sessions or use them during group sessions. Questions to guide your study can spark discussion of Psalms 1–50's key points and truths to be discovered in these profound psalms.

LIST OF MARGIN ICONS USED IN PSALMS 1–50

 Shepherd's Notes. Placed at the end of each section, a capsule statement provides the reader with the essence of the message of that section.

 Historical Context. To indicate historical information—historical, biographical, cultural—and provide insight on the understanding or interpretation of a passage.

 Old Testament Reference. Used when the writer refers to Old Testament passages or when Old Testament passages illuminate a text.

 New Testament Reference. Used when the writer refers to New Testament passages that are either fulfilled prophecy, an antitype of an Old Testament type, or a New Testament text which in some other way illuminates the passages under discussion.

 Personal Application. Used when the text provides a personal or universal application of truth.

 Word Picture. Indicates that the meaning of a specific word or phrase is illustrated so as to shed light on it.

The book of Psalms or the *Psalter* is the hymnal of Israelite worship and the Bible's book of personal devotions. In it we not only find expression of all the emotions of life but also some of the most profound teaching in the entire Bible.

DATE AND AUTHORSHIP OF THE PSALMS

The Psalter was not completed until late in Israelite history (in the postexilic era). But it contains hymns written over a period of hundreds of years.

Evidence of the superscriptions. A primary source of information regarding the date and authorship of individual psalms are the superscriptions found above many psalms. According to these, some of the authors include David, the sons of Korah, Asaph, Moses, and Solomon. Other psalms, including some of the "Psalms of Ascent" (Pss. 120–134) and "Hallelujah" psalms (Pss. 146–150) are anonymous. These superscriptions, if taken at face value, would date many of the psalms to the early tenth century (psalms of David) and at least one to the fifteenth century (Ps. 90).

Meaning and reliability of the superscriptions. Some scholars, however, question whether the superscriptions are meant to ascribe authorship to the Psalms. A more serious question is whether the superscriptions are reliable. Some scholars believe they were added at a late date and are no more than conjectures that have no real historical value. But there are good reasons to believe the superscriptions can be trusted.

The phrase *ledawid* used frequently in the psalm superscriptions could mean "by David" or "for David." But the clause following the superscription to Psalm 18 favors "by David."

Many of the psalm superscriptions refer to incidents in the life of David about which Samuel and Chronicles say nothing. For example, the superscription of Psalm 60 mentions battles with Aram-Naharaim, Aram-Zobah, and Edom. It would be strange if, in the late postexilic period, rabbis invented this. Another example is the superscription of Psalm 7, which speaks of a certain "Cush the Benjamite" (he is mentioned only here in the Old Testament). If the superscriptions were late fabrications, one would expect that they would refer more to incidents from David's life mentioned in Samuel.

Many of the psalm superscriptions contain technical musical terms, the meanings of which were already lost by the time the Old Testament was translated into Greek. For example, *lammenasseah*, the word which means "for the choir leader," is wrongly translated "to the end" in the Septuagint, the pre-Christian Greek translation of the Old Testament. A number of these terms are still not understood.

Obscure or difficult words in the superscriptions include:

- *Song Titles:* "Do Not Destroy"; "A Dove on Distant Oaks"; "The Doe of the Morning"; "Lilies"; "The Lilies of the Covenant"; and "Mahalath"
- *Musical Instruments* or *Technical Terms:* "stringed instruments" and "Sheminith"
- *Musical Guilds* or *Singers:* "Asaph"; "Sons of Korah"; "Heman the Ezrahite"; "Ethan the Ezrahite"
- *Types of Psalms:* "Songs of Ascent," likely sung by those who were making a pilgrimage to Jerusalem; *maskil,* possibly an instructional or meditative psalm.

Ancient terminology and references to old guilds and bygone events all imply that the titles are very old. This supports confidence in their reliability.

Davidic authorship of Psalms. Many scholars have asserted that David did not write the Psalms attributed to him. But there are no historical reasons why David could not have authored those Psalms. David had a reputation as a singer and as a devoted servant of the Lord, and nothing in his life is incompatible with his being a psalmist.

One difficulty that has been raised is that some of the Psalms of David seem to refer to the Temple (for example, 27:4), which did not exist in his day. But terms like "house of the Lord," "holy place," and "house of God" are regularly used of the tent of meeting and need not be taken as references to Solomon's Temple (see Exod. 28:43; 29:30; Josh. 6:24).

Other psalms that mention the Temple, however, are also ascribed to David (Pss. 5; 11; 18; 27; 29; 65; 68; 138). The word *temple* (*hêhal*) does not necessarily refer to Solomon's Temple. The word *hêkal* is used in 1 Samuel 1:9; 3:3 of the tabernacle. It also refers sometimes to God's dwelling place as in 2 Samuel 22:7. In Psalm 27 God's house is called "house," "temple," "booth," and "tent."

The date of the Psalms. Earlier critics dated many of the Psalms late in Israel's history, some as late as the Maccabean period. For two reasons, however, this is no longer possible.

First, the Ugaritic songs and hymns show parallels to many of the Psalms. The grammar and poetic forms are similar. The Ugaritic tradition of hymn writing is ancient (before the twelfth

Ugarit was an important city in Syria whose excavation has provided tablets giving closest primary evidence available for reconstructing the Canaanite religion that was a perennial temptation to Israel.

13

century B.C.) and implies that many of the Psalms may be ancient too.

Second, a fragmentary, second-century B.C. copy of the biblical collection of Psalms was found in the Dead Sea Scrolls. This proves beyond doubt that the Psalms were composed well before the second century B.C., since it must have taken a long time for the written Psalms to be recognized as Scripture and for the Psalter to be organized.

There is no reason, therefore, to date all the Psalms late. Generally speaking, they can be dated to three broad periods: (1) *Preexilic.* This would include those Psalms that are very much like the Ugaritic songs, the royal psalms, and those that mention the Northern Kingdom. (2) *Exilic.* This would include the dirge songs that lament the fall of Jerusalem and call for vengeance on the Edomites and others. (3) *Early postexilic.* This would include Psalms that emphasize the written law, such as Psalm 119.

THE COMPILATION OF THE PSALMS

Psalms divides into five sections or "books":

Book One:	Psalms 1–41
Book Two:	Psalms 42–72
Book Three:	Psalms 73–89
Book Four:	Psalms 90–106
Book Five:	Psalms 107–150

We have no precise information regarding the dates when the five books of the Psalms were compiled or what the criteria of compilation were. Psalm 72:20 implies that a compilation of David's psalms was made shortly after his death.

In Hezekiah's time there were collections of the psalms of David and Asaph, which may account for the bulk of the first three books (2 Chron. 29:30). At a later date another scribe may have collected the remaining books of the Psalter. Psalms was put into its final form some time in the postexilic period.

The five books each close with a doxology, and Psalm 150 is a concluding doxology for the entire Psalter. But the numbering of the Psalms varies. The Jerusalem Talmud speaks of 147 psalms. The Septuagint divides Psalms 116 and 147 into two psalms each but numbers Psalms 9 and 10 and Psalms 114 and 115 as one psalm each.

King Hezekiah and his officials ordered the Levites to praise the Lord with the words of David and of Asaph the seer. So they sang praises with gladness and bowed their heads and worshiped (2 Chron. 29:30).

TYPES OF PSALMS

When studying a psalm, one should ask the following questions: (1) Was it sung by an individual or the congregation? (2) What was the psalm's purpose (praise, cry for help, thanksgiving, admonition)? (3) Does it mention any special themes, such as the royal house or Zion? By asking these questions, scholars have identified a number of psalm types.

Hymns. In this type of psalm, the whole congregation praises God for His works or attributes (Ps. 105). Six subcategories of hymns are:

Victory songs, which praise God for His victories over the nations (Ps. 68);

Processional hymns, sung as the worshipers moved into the temple area (Ps. 24);

Zion songs which praise God and specifically refer to His presence in Zion (Ps. 48);

Songs of the *Lord's reign,* which include the words, "The Lord reigns" (Ps. 99);

Antiphonal hymns chanted by either the priests or choir with the congregation responding antiphonally (Ps. 136); and

Hallelujah hymns, which begin or end with "Praise the Lord!" (Hebrew, *hallelu Yah;* Ps. 146).

Community complaints. In these psalms the whole nation voiced its complaints over problems it was facing, such as defeat in battle, famine, or drought (Ps. 74). A subcategory of this is the *national imprecation,* in which the people cursed their oppressors as enemies of Israel's God (Ps. 83).

Individual complaints. These psalms are like the community complaint except that they were prayers given by one person instead of the whole nation. The reason for the prayers might be that the individual was sick, hounded by enemies, or in need of confessing personal sin (Ps. 13). This type of psalm may include substantial *imprecation* or curses against the psalmist's personal enemies (Ps. 5). A subcategory is the *penitential psalm,* in which the speaker is dominated by a sense of guilt (Ps. 51).

Individual songs of thanksgiving. In these psalms an individual praises God for some saving act. Usually it alludes to a time that the individual was sick or in some other kind of trouble (Ps. 116).

Royal psalms. These psalms deal with the king and the royal house. Subcategories include:

Wedding songs, sung at the marriage of the king (Ps. 45);

Coronation songs (Ps. 72);

Prayers for victory, chanted when the king went to war (Ps. 20); and

Votive psalms, perhaps sung by the king at his coronation as a vow to be faithful and upright (Ps. 101).

Torah psalms. These psalms give moral or religious instruction (Pss. 1; 127). Subcategories include:

Testimony songs in which the psalmist used his personal experience of God's salvation to encourage the hearer (Ps. 32); and

Wisdom songs, in which the psalmist instructed the hearer more in practical wisdom similar to that in Proverbs than in the law (Ps. 49).

Oracle psalms. These psalms report a decree of God (Ps. 82). The content of the oracle is often divine judgment, and the psalm concludes with a prayer for God to carry out His decree. But see also Psalm 87, an oracle of salvation for the Gentiles

Blessing psalms. In these psalms a priest pronounces a blessing upon the hearer(s) (Ps. 128).

Taunt songs. These psalms reproach the godless for their vile behavior and promise that their doom is near (Ps. 52).

Songs of trust. In these psalms the psalmist may face difficulty but remains assured of God's help and proclaims his faith and trust (Ps. 11).

When interpreting a psalm, it is important first to determine what kind of psalm it is. In this way one can see how the psalmist intended it to be read. (See article at the back of this book, "Types of Old Testament Literature.")

Torah is a Hebrew word normally translated "law" which eventually became a title for the Pentateuch, the first five books of the Old Testament.

THEOLOGICAL SIGNIFICANCE OF THE PSALMS

The Psalms help today's believers to understand God, themselves, and their relationship to God. The Psalms picture God as the Creator, who is worthy of praise and is capable of using His creative might to rescue His people from current distress. The Psalms picture God as the just Judge of all the world who rewards the righteous and opposes the wicked.

Prayers that God should curse the enemies of the psalmist must be understood in part as affirmations of God's justice and the certainty of His judgment. The Psalms picture God as the faithful friend of the oppressed. The Psalms offer a refresher course in God's faithfulness throughout Israel's history. The Psalms highlight God's promises to David and his descendants, promises that are not finally realized until Christ.

The Psalms picture the full range of human emotions: joy, despair, guilt, consolation, love, hate, thankfulness, and dissatisfaction. The Psalms thus remind us that all of life is under God's lordship. The Psalms likewise illustrate the broad range of human responses to God: praise, confession, pleas for help, thanksgiving. The Psalms thus serve as a sourcebook for Christian worship, both public and private.

THE FAITH OF THE PSALMS

As noted, the Psalms set forth the basic faith of the Hebrew people. God and man are the two basic focal points of that faith. These were the two inescapable realities. A religion which loses sight of either has failed to meet human needs. Their ancient faith also had two basic emphases: human need and divine providence. The Hebrew people were overwhelmingly aware

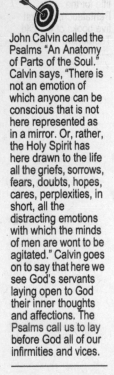

John Calvin called the Psalms "An Anatomy of Parts of the Soul." Calvin says, "There is not an emotion of which anyone can be conscious that is not here represented as in a mirror. Or, rather, the Holy Spirit has here drawn to the life all the griefs, sorrows, fears, doubts, hopes, cares, perplexities, in short, all the distracting emotions with which the minds of men are wont to be agitated." Calvin goes on to say that here we see God's servants laying open to God their inner thoughts and affections. The Psalms call us to lay before God all of our infirmities and vices.

that the plight of humanity was quite desperate as they faced the problems of sin, guilt, and evil. They were equally certain that God was sovereign, His purposes were good, and He would ultimately be victorious. The consequences of the divine sovereignty brought to the hearts and the lips of the Hebrews both praise and thanksgiving. They praised God for what He was and thanked Him for what He had done.

Finally, the faith of the psalmists can be characterized as having four dimensions. They always looked back to the past, to God's great acts of creation and more especially to His great acts of redemption and deliverance. In the present dimension of their faith, they were aware that God was with them, even when they did not "feel" His presence. Where they were, He was. Because of what God had done and because of their present experience with Him, they could look forward to being in His presence in the future. This gave them hope. The fourth dimension to the faith of the psalmists was timelessness. Their faith transcended time and speaks to the hearts of all people everywhere. This makes the book of Psalms a universal favorite among people. Wherever we are in our spiritual pilgrimage, we can find psalms which express our deepest thoughts, our greatest hopes, and our utmost certainties.

THE PSALMS FOR BELIEVERS TODAY

The list of teachings we gain from Psalms has no end. Its 150 songs call us to pray, to praise, to confess, and to testify. The prayer path to God is open at all times for all people in all situations. At all times we should take our feelings to God. He hears and accepts us. In His own way He answers. He brings salvation to our lives. Sin plagues each of us. We rebel against God's way.

God waits for us to confess our sins. He does not give us our deserts.

He forgives, redeems, and renews our lives. We may not be able to sing. We can praise God. We need to be aware of the great acts He is accomplishing in our lives and the great things He has accomplished for us in creation and in His saving actions through Jesus Christ. Knowing He acts for us, we can rejoice and praise Him at all times. We have no monopoly on God. He has chosen to help all nations praise Him. We must daily testify to others what God has done for us.

Background: Psalm 1 is the prologue to the entire Psalter. It is a preface poem to introduce the hymnbook of the Hebrew faith.

The Hebrew language uses two expressions for negative statements: *immediate* and *permanent* prohibitions. The following three negatives are *permanent prohibitions* that refer to actions that are never to take place in the life of the believer. The righteous person: (1) does not take the advice of evil men for his guide, (2) does not hang out with those who are habitual moral failures, and (3) does not become one who scorns the sacred and mocks God.

PSALM 1: IN SEARCH OF HAPPINESS

Theme: The two ways
Reader insights: A wisdom song. This psalm accurately reflects classic Old Testament theology: the righteous prosper and the wicked perish. The basic premise of the psalm is the happiness of the righteous and the ruin of the wicked. The righteous are friends of God who live in obedience to His covenant. The wicked are enemies of God who rebel against His will.

PSALM SUMMARY

Happy is the righteous person (1:1). The psalmist begins with a beatitude—an invocation of blessing and congratulations. It could be translated, "O how happy is the person who . . . " He then describes (1) what the righteous person *does not* do; and (2) what the righteous person *does*.

What the righteous person does (1:2–3). On the positive side, the righteous person finds delight in the law of the Lord (v. 2). The righteous person's joy is to meditate on the teachings of Scripture and the revealed will of God.

The disastrous fate of the wicked (1:4–5). Verse 4 begins emphatically, "Not so the wicked!" They are like worthless chaff blown away by the wind. Note the contrast of chaff with the stability of the tree planted by streams of water.

■ *The psalmist contrasts the ways of the righ-*
■ *teous and the wicked. The way of the righ-*
■ *teous leads to God and eternal life; the way*
■ *of the wicked leads to ruin and death.*

Wheat was threshed by beating it on a hard surface to dislodge the grain. It was then tossed into the air. The heavy grain would fall back to the ground. But the light chaff or husks would be blown away by the wind. They were considered worthless. The wicked are just as unstable.

GUIDING QUESTIONS

How is the righteous person like a tree? How is the wicked person like chaff?

PSALM 2: THE LAUGHTER OF GOD

Theme: The coronation of a king

Reader insights: A royal psalm. Christians would later apply this psalm to the ideal King, the Messiah, who is the Son of David. It is one of the most quoted and alluded to psalms in the New Testament.

PSALM SUMMARY

Plotting against the new king (2:1–3). "Why do the nations conspire?" (v. 1). This is not a question so much as an expression of astonishment that the nations are planning a revolt.

But God makes promises to the new king (2:4–9). God laughs at the futile schemes of His enemies.

Background: This psalm was composed for the coronation of Israel's kings. It may have been recited by the king himself and appears to be based on Nathan's oracle in 2 Samuel 7:8–16.

When a new king came to the throne, vassal nations under Israel's rule would plot revolt. This afforded them an ideal time for breaking away. The psalmist, however, was mystified at their futile conspiracy (v. 1).

He sees their rebellion as being against the Lord, as well as against his "anointed" (literally "Messiah"). Davidic kings were given the title "anointed." After the end of the monarchy in 586 B.C., the term was used to refer to the ideal future king or Messiah. Peter quoted this passage in his sermon at Pentecost (see Acts 4:25–29).

Background: This is the first in a series of psalms attributed to King David (Pss. 3–41). The psalm's setting is believed to be David's flight before the army of Absalom, his rebellious son (2 Sam. 15–19). The psalm was probably used by both David and his successors.

Those who rebel against God's "anointed" face His severe judgment (v. 9).

An exhortation to submit (2:10–11). The psalmist (and the new king) sounds a warning to the rebels (v. 10). They are to serve the Lord reverently and respectfully lest they perish (v. 11).

■ *God sits in heaven and laughs at the folly of*
■ *rebellious people. Those who rebel against*
■ *God's "anointed" will be met with God's*
■ *judgment. We find in this passage an impor-*
■ *tant messianic reference: the king is God's*
■ *son. We know from the New Testament that*
■ *Jesus is God's unique Son.*

GUIDING QUESTION

Why is this psalm considered to be a messianic psalm?

PSALM 3: GOD IS OUR SHIELD

Theme: Faith in God, who hears our prayers and protects us from threatening evil

Reader insights: Although sometimes classified as a psalm of lament, Psalm 3 is really a protective psalm. Known as a morning psalm, it goes with Psalm 4, which is an evening psalm.

PSALM SUMMARY

Plight (3:1–2). The psalmist pours out his heart to God in distress over his enemies who mock his reliance on God (v. 2).

Unwavering confidence in God in the midst of danger (3:3–6). In this increasingly perilous situation, the psalmist affirms that God is his shield, God answers prayer, God will sustain him. Therefore, there is no reason to fear even tens of thousands. The psalmist's cry, "Arise, O LORD!" is thought to be the ancient battle cry of Israel's army. Here the psalmist pleads for deliverance.

- *The psalmist fully trusts in God. In the midst*
- *of his trouble, God sustains him and banishes*
- *his fear.*

GUIDING QUESTIONS

What is the background for this psalm? What additional details can we learn from 2 Samuel 15–19?

PSALM 4: THE HAPPY HEART

Theme: Trust in God despite adverse circumstances

Reader insights: An individual lament. Considered to be an evening psalm. It begins with a plea for help (v. 1), but turns out to be a strong affirmation of personal faith. Sincere faith in God is a source of comfort and peace, whatever outward circumstances may be.

PSALM SUMMARY

A plea to God and God's answer (4:1–3). The psalmist is in trouble, but he does not despair. He is confident, basing his trust on past experiences in which God has answered his prayers.

Background: This is the first of fifty-five psalms with instructions to the choirmaster in its title, "with stringed instruments." This probably called for a quiet musical background for the reading or singing of the psalm in public worship. The stringed instruments would likely include the lyre and harp (Pss. 150:3; 49:4).

The apostle Paul quoted verse 4 in his practical exhortation in Ephesians 4:26: "Do not let the sun go down while you are still angry." Nursed anger is self-destructive.

The psalmist advises his enemies to trust in God (4:4–6). The psalmist's enemies are ridiculing him. They busy themselves chasing delusions which do not satisfy their soul hunger. The psalmist urges his followers to handle their anger wisely and to trust God. He shows awareness of complaints that are being expressed among God's people.

The joy of a happy heart (4:7–8). In the midst of these complaints he boldly asks for God's blessing and turns to God with a heart overflowing with thanks. He closes by saying that even in the midst of these life-threatening circumstances, he can lie down and sleep soundly.

■ *In contrast to the doubts and anxieties*
■ *expressed by his enemies, the psalmist sings*
■ *about joy and peace during adversity.*

GUIDING QUESTIONS
In the midst of his trouble, how did the psalmist pray to God? What did he want God to do for him?

PSALM 5: WORDS AND SIGNS

Theme: A morning prayer for protection

Reader insights: An individual lament. While it is a plea for deliverance from enemies, it is even more an affirmation of the worshiper's faith.

PSALM SUMMARY

The morning petition (5:1–3). Of the appointed times for worship at the Temple, the morning seemed to be the most important. The psalmist prays repeatedly, "Give ear ... consider ... hear." He expresses God's hatred of evil. He doesn't claim to be perfect but says because of God unfailing love, he can enter the Temple to worship—to stand in awe of God. He expresses a fervent desire to know clearly and to do exactly what God wants him to do.

Prayer regarding enemies (5:4–12). The psalmist next complains to God about his enemies—especially their destructive speech which consists of lies and flattery. He urges God to indict them and let them experience the consequences of their destructive behavior. He also asks God to get them away from him. The psalmist turns from God's enemies to those who seek God's protection. For these, the psalmist asks protection, joy, a sense of great security.

Background: This psalm is a morning prayer. It would have been sung in the Temple at dawn as the morning sacrifice was offered.

There are numerous references to morning prayer in the Psalms (see 88:13).

In verse 1 the psalmist speaks of "my words" and "my sighings." The latter word may refer to his stammering or halting prayer. It is also translated, "Consider my inmost thoughts" (NEB).

■ *After describing the character of his enemies,*
■ *the psalmist closes this section with praise*
■ *for God's grace and protection.*

25

GUIDING QUESTIONS

What is the character of the psalmist's enemies? What warning does he give them?

PSALM 6: A PRAYER FOR HEALING

Theme: A prayer for healing during a sickness
Reader insights: An individual lament. This is the first of the "seven penitential psalms" often used in Christian worship (see also Pss. 32; 38; 51; 102; 130; 143).

PSALM SUMMARY

A prayer for healing (6:1–7). The psalmist is sick in both body and soul. He views his illness as coming from the hand of God with his enemies as agents of God's discipline. He doesn't make excuses for himself but cries out for healing on the basis of God's unfailing love. He reminds God that those in the grave, in Sheol, can no longer praise God. To paraphrase, "What good will I be to You when I'm dead?"

Confidence in answered prayer (6:8–10). The tone of the psalm changes abruptly. The psalmist experiences healing. God hears and answers his prayer, delivering him from sickness unto death. Like Job's comforters, his enemies had troubled him. Now he is vindicated before them.

Background: The title calls for the singing of this psalm to be accompanied with stringed instruments.

In Old Testament times, suffering was generally thought to be caused by sin. Often we suffer because of sin, but not always. Sometimes the innocent suffer, which is the theme of the book of Job (see also John 9:1–3).

■ *God answers his prayer, and the psalmist*
■ *experiences healing. He is now vindicated*
■ *before his enemies.*

GUIDING QUESTION

What is the outcome of the psalmist's desperate situation?

PSALM 7: GOD, THE RIGHTEOUS JUDGE

Theme: The prayer of a person falsely accused
Reader insights: The psalmist laments his enemies' accusations and declares his oath of innocence.

PSALM SUMMARY

Cry for deliverance (7:1–2). The writer states his faith in God and pleads for deliverance. The psalmist's enemies are like a dangerous lion that will destroy him (v. 2).

Declaration of innocence (7:3–5). Having been accused of dishonesty, the writer calls on God to curse him if he is guilty. He is not claiming moral perfection, but simply insists on his innocence concerning his enemies' accusations. If he is guilty of wrong, he prays that God would let his enemies overtake him, trample him, and make him sleep in the dust.

God, the righteous judge (7:6–11). The psalmist asks God to hold court and establish his integrity. He knows justice is on his side because he is not guilty. Those who refuse to repent incur God's wrath and judgment.

The boomerang of evil (7:12–16). God is depicted as using a soldier's weapons: a sharp sword, powerful bow, and fiery arrows (vv. 12–13). The evil person (v. 14) is pregnant with mischief and gives birth to lies (see James 1:13–15). But

In the Psalms, *salvation* most often means deliverance from peril. That basic concept is later expanded to include spiritual salvation from the power of evil.

27

evil attitudes and actions backfire. An evil person digs a trap for someone else and "falls into the pit he has made" (v. 15).

A vow (7:17). The final verse is a sacred promise of praise. The writer declares that he will not fail to be grateful for his deliverance.

Lessons in living: In difficult times we need to trust God and allow Him to use these times to test for our obedience to His instruction or for developing specific areas of our lives.

■ *The psalmist declares his innocence and calls*
■ *on God to curse him if he is guilty of wrong.*
■ *God is the righteous Judge. Those who refuse*
■ *to repent incur His wrath and judgment.*

GUIDING QUESTION

Why is the psalmist so confident that God will vindicate him?

Background: David was moved to praise by the starry heavens above and the dignity of man.

PSALM 8: WHAT IS MAN?

Theme: The greatness of God and man's place in the universe
Reader insights: A hymn. This psalm is the creation story set to music.

PSALM SUMMARY

The praise of children (8:1–2). This psalm begins and ends with adoration of God who has taught even children to praise Him. Children's praise of God has the effect of silencing His enemies.

God's glory in creation (8:3–4). In light of the vast expansiveness of space, humans appear insignificant (v. 4). When we consider all of creation, we are but a speck of cosmic dust—but we are thinking specks, made in the image of our Creator.

What is man? (8:4). This is the haunting question of the ages. Every philosopher, theologian, and thinking person has asked this question. The paradox is apparent. Compared to the universe, humans seem insignificant. Yet, because we are made in the image of God, we have great worth and potential for fellowship with our Maker.

Man, the crown of creation (8:5–8). "The son of man" (mere, mortal man) is made in the likeness of God. This title was used in the New Testament of Jesus as representative of humanity. Man is crowned (encircled) with glory and honor and given dominion over creation (Gen. 1:26f.). Man has dominated creation, from taming wild horses to harnessing the atom, thereby fulfilling the divine command.

- *Man is crowned (encircled) with glory and*
- *honor and given dominion over creation.*
- *Creating humans in His own image, God*
- *made us "a little lower than God"*

GUIDING QUESTION
What might have been David's inspiration for writing this psalm?

Background: This hymn of praise is for a national victory over enemies of which the historical background may be 2 Samuel 8.

PSALM 9: PROTECTOR OF THE POOR

Theme: God is the champion of the poor and needy

Reader insights: Psalms 9 and 10 were originally one psalm and are so translated in ancient Greek and Latin. They have a common alphabetical framework. An acrostic is used with lines of the two psalms beginning with the letters of the Hebrew alphabet. Psalm 9 is a hymn of praise, and Psalm 10 is a lament.

PSALM SUMMARY

A call to thanksgiving (9:1–4). God's wonderful acts are a cause for praise and thanksgiving. These include His mighty acts on behalf of His people Israel (vv. 1–2). The psalmist has personally found God acting on his behalf, as well (vv. 3–4).

A hymn of praise (9:5–14). God is the righteous Judge of both mankind and nations. His judgment is final. God is securely enthroned and judges "with justice" (vv. 7–8). He is the believer's stronghold (vv. 9–10). His faithfulness calls forth praise (vv. 11–12).

In verses 13–14 the psalmist again sounds a personal petition, like that in verses 1–4. He asked to be spared at "the gates of death."

Judgment on the nations (9:15–20). Nations that forget God find themselves ensnared in their own evil devices (vv. 15–16). They go down to the abode of the dead (Sheol, v. 17). The final verse in this psalm is a potent prayer, "Let the nations know they are but men!" The psalmist reassures his readers that God is indeed the champion of the poor and needy. They will not be overlooked or allowed to perish (v. 18).

𝕾

■ *God will judge those who forget Him. God's*
■ *judgment is not reserved exclusively for the*
■ *future; He may choose to pass judgment on*
■ *the wicked at any time.*

GUIDING QUESTION

From this psalm, what do we learn about the nature of God's judgment?

PSALM 10: THE WAY THE WICKED THINK

Background: The psalmist is troubled by the apparent absence of God and is greatly troubled by His silence.

Theme: Lament over the arrogance of the wicked
Reader insight: A song of trust.

PSALM SUMMARY

The absence of God (10:1–2). The psalmist is troubled by God's apparent absence. The Almighty seems to be in hiding, allowing the wicked to enjoy a field day.

The boasts of the wicked (10:3–13). God's apparent absence made the wicked bold. Morally and intellectually misguided, they make several false boasts about God.

But God does see (10:14–18). He never sleeps and is always caring. The helpless ("fatherless") trust in him and will not be disappointed (v. 14). In due course God will punish the evildoer (v. 15). Nations come and go, but God remains. He is the one constant in the midst of change. God will hear the prayer of the meek and deliver the oppressed (vv. 17–18). They will not always have to live in terror. How different are the judgments of God! He looks on the intention of the heart and judges fairly. He does not run His world on our timetable.

- *The wicked have completely misread God.*
- *He is always aware and never sleeps. He*
- *looks on the intention of the heart and*
- *judges fairly. In due course God will punish*
- *evildoers.*

GUIDING QUESTIONS

The psalmist is troubled by God's apparent absence. Why do you believe God allows these times? What is the proper response when this happens in a believer's spiritual walk?

PSALM 11: "FLEE LIKE A BIRD"

Theme: Trust in God in spite of apparently hopeless circumstances
Reader insight: A song of trust.

PSALM SUMMARY

Faith over fear (11:1–3). The psalmist has taken refuge in the Lord. His faith is even more vivid when seen against the backdrop of his friends' fear. Moral foundations were crumbling (v. 3). The psalmist was fighting for a lost cause, in a hopeless situation. Still, he affirms his unshaken faith in God.

But God (11:4–7). We see a contrast between the psalmist and his friends. The psalmist's friends were looking at outward circumstances and feeling despair. He, instead, is looking in faith toward God and is confident. God observes all we do (v. 5). He tests and proves both the righteous and the wicked. His test is like the refiner's

Background: The psalmist is in danger and is advised to "flee like a bird to your mountain" (v. 1). But he will not take refuge in the hill country. Though his cause appears hopeless, he affirms his faith in God.

God is the believer's refuge. This truth is characteristic of many of the Psalms (see Pss. 7; 16; 31; 57; 71).

fire which separates gold from base metals. His judgment will be tough (v. 6). Those who do right will see God's face.

■ *These verses are the psalmist's reply to his*
■ *friends, who had advised him to flee to the*
■ *mountains. The psalmist asserts his confi-*
■ *dence in God, declaring that God is still in*
■ *control, He observes all we do, and tries both*
■ *the upright and the wicked.*

GUIDING QUESTIONS

What are the circumstances surrounding the psalmist's decision to take refuge in God? How relevant is the psalmist's situation to the modern–day believer?

PSALM 12: GOD'S PURE PROMISES

Theme: Human flattery and faithful words
Reader insight: A community lament.

PSALM SUMMARY

The psalmist's cry for help (12:1–4). In the psalmist's day, godly people were few and far between (v. 1). Those in positions of leadership were liars and guilty of flattery. Someone has said that flattery is like perfume: it's OK if you sniff it, but dangerous if you swallow it. These braggarts are deliberately deceiving others (v. 2).

The ungodly speak with mixed motives—a double heart. They have a hidden agenda and follow an evil purpose (v. 4). It is a time of social

"Double heart"

The NIV's rendering "with deception" (v. 2) is literally "with a double heart" in the Hebrew text.

corruption; people cannot be trusted. They have perverted the gift of speech for selfish ends.

God's bright promises (12:5–6). God promises to come to the aid of the poor and needy who are oppressed: "I will protect them" (v. 5). The promises of God are as pure and precious as silver refined seven times (the number for perfection or thoroughness). The psalmist is here contrasting the trustworthy word of God with the flattery and lies of people.

■ *The psalmist sounds a cry for help. Honest*
■ *people have disappeared, and flattery is the*
■ *rule. Wicked people are speaking fine-sound-*
■ *ing words that are void of substance.*

GUIDING QUESTIONS

Describe the speech of the wicked. What are its characteristics?

PSALM 13: DARK AND DAWN

Theme: A desperate plea for God's deliverance
Reader insight: An individual lament.

PSALM SUMMARY

Background: The setting of this psalm may be a time of sickness or the threat of a taunting enemy. It uses a common biblical theme: darkness and light, tragedy and triumph.

"How long, O Lord?" (13:1–2). The psalmist repeats his strong lament four times in the form of a question: "How long?" He feels forgotten and abandoned by God. He feels pain in his soul and has a sorrowful heart (v. 2). His enemies are in triumph.

The psalmist may appear harsh in his complaint, but we can see that he is being honest with God. He is not guilty of any false piety that he uses to cover his true feelings. God respects the prayers of honest souls and answers the prayers of desperate ones.

A plea for God to answer (13:3–4). The psalmist now pleads for God to answer him. If God does not come to his aid, he might "sleep the sleep of death" and his enemies might take that as proof they were right. The Bible often speaks of death as sleep (see Job 3:13 and 1 Thess. 4:14).

An affirmation of trust (13:5–6). Despite the darkness, the psalmist lives in anticipation of the dawn. He trusts in God's steadfast love and knows that he will not be disappointed. He promises to rejoice and to sing to the Lord for answered prayer (v. 6). Despite his loneliness, the psalmist's faith is unshaken. Faith knows that God will have the last word. And faith expects it to be a good word. God gives us our song back and restores the joy of our salvation. Martin Luther said, "Hope despairs and yet despair hopes."

■ *The psalmist makes a strong plea for God to*
■ *answer him. He follows that plea with an*
■ *affirmation of trust in God's steadfast love.*

GUIDING QUESTION
This psalm can be divided into three parts. How do you describe each part?

Lessons in living: When your cry becomes, "How long, O Lord," do your best to align with His timing and rest on the promises of His Word.

Background: This a reflective psalm that describes the lot of God's people in a godless world.

An important part of this psalm is repeated in Romans 3:10–12. Paul tells the bad news about human nature that must be acknowledged, but human beings have hope through God's grace.

Lessons in living: The most foolish thing a person can do is leave God out of his or her life. We must resolve never to make the mistake of the fool. Proverbs puts it clearly: "In all your ways acknowledge him, and he will make your paths straight" (3:6).

Theme: A meditation about the fool

Reader insights: An oracle psalm. Psalm 14 is repeated almost entirely in the course of the book of Psalms, and Psalm 53 is nearly an exact duplication.

PSALM SUMMARY

The "fool" (14:1–3). The fool believes that God is not One to be reckoned with. He may not deny God with his lips, but he lives life without reference to God. As a consequence, he does evil.

God will judge (14:4–7). But the fool's decision has as little effect on God as a person in a dark room denying that the sun exists. God doesn't miss a thing. His gaze is so accurate that to His pure eyes there is no one who is right. God asks if these fools who do evil will ever come to their senses. The implied answer is that they never will. As a result, they are in for a surprise. Facing God whom they have denied will be a time of terror. In contrast, God will be on the side of those who obey Him.

- *The fool lives his life as if God did not exist.*
- *He will discover the error of his ways when*
- *God's judgement comes upon all who mis-*
- *treat His people.*

GUIDING QUESTION

What does the psalmist mean by a "fool"?

PSALM 15: GUESTS OF GOD

Theme: Preparation for worship

PSALM SUMMARY

The question (15:1). "Who is permitted to come into the sanctuary to worship the Lord?"

The qualifications (15:2–5). The rest of the psalm is given to answering that question. Many of the requirements have to do with the use of the tongue:

Background: This psalm was used by Jewish pilgrims entering the Temple to worship. They would ask the question in verse 1 at the entrance. From inside the Temple courtyard, priests would answer (vv. 2–5).

CONDITIONS OF THE UPRIGHT PERSON

Positive (v. 2)

Walks blamelessly

Does what is right

Speaks the truth

Negative (v. 3)

No slander

No evil

No reproach

Negative (v. 4)

Despises reprobates

Keeps oaths

Positive (v. 5)

No usury

No bribery

The worshiper is considered the guest of God, enjoying divine hospitality (cp. Ps. 23:5–6, where the Lord is portrayed as the psalmist's host).

Background: This appears to be a prayer for protection in a crisis. It is possible that this psalm began as an inscription on a monument celebrating a specific deliverance from a crisis.

The list in this psalm is not exhaustive but representative of the highly ethical demands of the Ten Commandments.

- *The person who may come into God's pres-*
- *ence must be one who is highly ethical, in*
- *both prayer and lifestyle. The psalmist goes*
- *on to present ten conditions for admission*
- *into the presence of the Almighty.*

GUIDING QUESTION

How might this psalm have been used in worship?

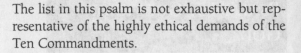

PSALM 16: GOD, MY REFUGE

Theme: Confidence in God in the face of death

PSALM SUMMARY

One true God (16:1–4). Here the psalmist is seeking safety. He begins by confessing that God is his Lord and is the source of all good. He prefers and looks up to God's people and avoids those who worship other gods.

Joy in the Lord (16:5–11). The psalmist values God above His gifts—specifically, the land God had given Israel. God guides and protects—even when the psalmist is asleep. Remembering this brings joy. Knowing God as he does, the psalmist does not fear death. He knows that the highest joy is being in God's presence and that this joy has no end—even in the face of death.

- *The psalmist rejoices in the Lord with his*
- *heart, soul, and body. This relationship gives*
- *him both security and joy.*

GUIDING QUESTION

The Hebrews seemed to battle the temptation to serve other gods. In what way might we see this kind of tendency today?

PSALM 17: A CRY FOR VINDICATION

Theme: A prayer for deliverance from unjust persecution

Reader insights: An individual lament. This is a very emotional prayer. The psalmist is as certain of the presence of God as in Psalm 16. He is protesting his innocence before false accusers.

PSALM SUMMARY

A plea for justice (17:1–2). This is a cry for vindication. The psalmist wants God to judge him to be right and his enemies to be wrong.

- *The psalmist wants to be heard. He cries out*
- *for vindication and justice.*

A declaration of innocence (17:3–5). God has tried the psalmist in a night prayer vigil. He has put him to the test and found no evil in him (v. 3). The psalmist has avoided violence and has walked faithfully in the right path.

Background: Portions of this psalm mirror the Song of the Sea in Exodus 15:1–8, in which Israel celebrated their deliverance from Pharaoh.

"The apple of your eye." The psalmist prays that God will keep him as "the apple of your eye." This is the pupil of the eye that is precious and is carefully guarded.

"In the shadow of your wings." The psalmist also prays to be kept "in the shadow of your wings." This could refer to the wings of the cherubim in the Temple; that is, in the divine presence. It may be a simple plea for protection, as a hen or eagle protects her chicks beneath her wings.

A request for divine protection (17:6–15). The psalmist prays confidently that God will hear and answer him (v. 6). He asks that God demonstrate His covenant love and be his Savior from enemies (v. 7), who are like hungry lions (v. 12). In verse 8 he uses two metaphors of divine protection: "the apple of your eye" and "in the shadow of your wings."

■ *The psalmist prays in confidence that God*
■ *will hear and answer his prayer. He asks*
■ *that God demonstrate His covenant love and*
■ *be his Savior from enemies. The psalmist*
■ *concludes with an expression of confidence.*
■ *He expects God to act on his behalf in the*
■ *morning.*

GUIDING QUESTION

What do the expressions "apple of your eye" and "shadow of your wings" mean?

PSALM 18: A ROYAL THANKSGIVING

Theme: Thanksgiving for victory over enemies
Reader insights: An individual song of thanksgiving. This mighty hymn is also found in 2 Samuel 22.

PSALM SUMMARY

Prelude to praise (18:1–3). This psalm opens with an expression of love to God, who is described in a number of rich metaphors: "my strength," "my rock," "my fortress," "my deliverer," "my shield," "my stronghold," "my God."

Background: This psalm celebrates King David's victory over his enemies. It was likely sung by succeeding Davidic kings in thanksgiving for other battles won. Additionally, it may have been used in one of Israel's great annual festivals, such as the Feast of Tabernacles.

Gratitude for divine deliverance (18:4–30). Next the psalmist recounts the extreme circumstances from which he called out to God for help (vv. 3–6). God's response to his prayer is awesome to behold (vv. 7–24). The psalmist articulates God's ways with human beings. He shows Himself faithful to those who are faithful. But He opposes those who are wicked.

A hymn celebrating victory (18:31–48). The king readily acknowledges God as the source of his victory, instead of taking personal credit for it. Only the Lord is God (v. 31). This God girds the king and makes him as secure as a mountain goat's feet are on the mountain heights. The king does his part in battle (vv. 37–38), yet he believes it is God who gives him the victory over his enemies (vv. 39–41). The result is that the defeated nations acknowledge the king's sovereignty (vv. 43–45) and pay homage to him.

The king then sings his grateful praise to the Lord (vv. 46–48), for God has proved to be his rock (his defense) and his salvation.

■ *The king acknowledges God as the source of*
■ *his victory, and sings praises to God for his*
■ *deliverance.*

GUIDING QUESTIONS

How did David celebrate his victory? How do you respond to the victories God gives you?

PSALM 19: GOD'S GLORY REVEALED IN NATURE AND LAW

Theme: The revelation of God in nature and in God's Word

Reader insights: A wisdom psalm. Both the created order and God's Word reveal His purpose for humanity. It is interesting that this psalm speaks of God's general revelation of Himself in creation and His special revelation in the Ten Commandments.

PSALM SUMMARY

God's glory revealed in nature (19:1–6). God's creation may not speak like human beings, but it does communicate to those who will listen. It is a powerful witness to His glory: the majestic heavens above, the continual transition from day to night, night to day, the sun in its daily course across the sky.

Note that the psalmist celebrated the glory of the sun and stars. Yet he did not worship them as gods, as did his neighbors in Egypt or Persia. Rather, they were part of creation and were made to glorify their Creator.

God's glory revealed in His Word (19:7–11). Creation shows an amazing lawlikeness. It is this characteristic of our world that makes it dependable. The same Creator who has so designed nature has a law for human beings, which, when followed, brings them great joy (vv. 7–11). To most of us, law is cold and uninspiring. But to the psalmist, it was exciting—something more exciting than money and sweeter than desserts that make our mouths water.

A prayer (19:12–14). The psalm closes with a prayer from the psalmist to have his sins exposed and cleansed and that he may, in the future, only say and think those things that are pleasing to God.

- ■ *In addition to nature, God has also revealed*
- ■ *Himself in His Word. These Scriptures reveal*
- ■ *what He is like and how He cares for His cre-*
- ■ *ation, including mankind. The psalmist then*
- ■ *uses a series of terms to describe the Law.*

GUIDING QUESTION

God has revealed Himself through both nature and His Word. How does each contribute to our revelation of Him?

PSALM 20: A PRAYER FOR VICTORY

Theme: Prayer for a king as he departs for battle

Reader insight: A prayer for victory and blessing.

PSALM SUMMARY

The people pray for their king's victory (20:1–5). The "name" of the Lord appears three times in this psalm (vv. 1, 5, 7). It is no magic formula assuring success. Rather, the name of God is a symbol of His self-revelation and His presence among His people.

The priest pronounces assurance of victory (20:6–8). Following the prayer of the people, the priest pronounces assurance of victory (vv. 6–8). Some might trust in mighty arms and other instruments of war. While these are important in battle, it is more important to trust

Background: The setting of this psalm was a royal worship service. A Davidic king was about to go into battle. He would pray and offer sacrifices (v. 3) and receive assurance of the Lord's help (see 1 Sam. 13:8–15). He, and the nation, needed God's presence and protection.

in the name of the Lord (v. 7). To trust in arms alone spells failure (v. 8; cp. Isa. 31:3).

God save the king (20:9). This concluding prayer sums up the theme of the psalm: "O Lord, save the king! Answer us when we call!" It is also a prayer for the nation, represented in the person of the king. The singing of this psalm was an occasion for strengthening the people's confidence in God, as well as for asking His help in battle.

- ■ *The worship leader proclaims the assurance*
- ■ *of victory. The Lord will give help to His*
- ■ *anointed king.*

GUIDING QUESTION

What is the occasion for this psalm?

Background: This is best understood as the sequel to Psalm 20. The battle has been fought and won. This is the hymn of thanksgiving for a successful military campaign.

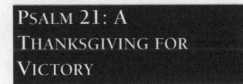

PSALM 21: A THANKSGIVING FOR VICTORY

Theme: A thanksgiving song for victory

Reader insights: Psalms 20 and 21 are royal psalms. The first is a prayer for victory in battle. This psalm is a prayer of thanksgiving for victory granted.

PSALM SUMMARY

Thanksgiving for answered prayer (21:1–7). God has helped the king. His heart's desire has been granted (v. 2). God has blessed the king with majesty as well as success in battle (v. 3). He has been granted long life (v. 4).

This promise of unending life applies to the dynasty and ultimately to the Messiah. The king knew both glory and gladness (vv. 5–6). The basis of his greatness is his trust in God's steadfast love (v. 7). The human side of that equation is *trust*. The divine side is *covenant love*.

Hope of future victories (21:8–12). War with neighboring tribes appears inevitable for Israel. Thus, it is essential that they rely on the Lord. Notice that the nation's enemies are also considered God's enemies. In verse 9 we probably have the description of a besieged city set on fire with its population still inside ("like a fiery furnace"). A broader application of this passage is God's final defeat of evil.

■ *God has answered the prayer of the people*
■ *and helped the king. Not only has the heart's*
■ *desire of the king been granted; he has also*
■ *been promised a long life. Wars with neigh-*
■ *boring nations will be inevitable, and Israel*
■ *asks that God not only "seize" their foes but*
■ *also destroy their descendants.*

A shout of praise (21:13). This concluding prayer was probably sung by the congregation. It has a future as well as a present reference. The church uses this psalm in its celebration of Christ's ascension. Christ has defeated the power of evil and has received glory from the Father.

GUIDING QUESTION
What is the background of this psalm?

PSALM 22: AGONY AND ECSTASY

Theme: Psalm of a person threatened with death
Reader insights: An individual lament. This is one of the most eloquent statements of human anguish in all literature. Yet it concludes with a declaration of faith and praise.

PSALM SUMMARY

The cry of anguish (22:1–21). The psalmist begins by expressing a profound sense of being abandoned by God. Even in his suffering and sense of abandonment, he realizes that God has delivered Israel in the past and that God reigns. This contrast between his own suffering and realization of who God is in some ways adds to his perplexity.

The psalmist (vv. 6–18) gives a graphic and detailed description of his situation. He calls out for the Lord's deliverance (vv. 19–21).

A hymn of praise (22:22–31). Suddenly, he sees beyond his pain. He praises God and urges those in his community of faith to join him. With prophetic insight, the psalmist looks ahead and glimpses the coming kingdom of God. He sees distant nations being converted to faith in God (v. 27). Even generations yet unborn enjoy His salvation (vv. 30–31). This has now come to pass. The psalm of anguish ends on a joyful note.

■ *The psalm changes direction from a cry of*
■ *anguish to a song of praise. The psalmist*
■ *vows to praise God for his deliverance and to*
■ *call on the congregation to join him. God*
■ *hears his cry.*

GUIDING QUESTION

Why is this psalm called the "Passion Psalm"?

PSALM 23: OUR SHEPHERD, OUR HOST

Theme: Psalm 23 reminds us that God is with us in the valley of deep darkness as well as in times of joy.

Reader insights: A song of trust. This is the psalm of psalms—the favorite of young and old alike. It is one of the best known and most loved passages in the Bible, second only to the Lord's Prayer. Psalm 22 is a song of deep anguish. Psalm 24 is a hymn of triumph. Psalm 23 is a bridge over troubled waters, joining the two.

Background: Imagine the setting when the shepherd David sang this psalm for the first time. It was a cold, starry night in Judea. The stars seemed so close he felt as though he could reach up and rake them down. The day of grazing and search for water was over. The sheep huddled asleep inside a thorn bush and stone enclosure. But the shepherd's work was not done. He had to keep a wary eye open for wild animals which threatened the sheep.

	PSALM 22	PSALM 23	PSALM 24
THEME:	Christ, the Good Shepherd	Christ, the Great Shepherd	Christ, the Chief Shepherd
MINISTRY:	Shepherd dies for His sheep	Shepherd cares for His sheep	Shepherd reigns over His sheep
KEY THOUGHT:	Anguish	Comfort	Triumph

PSALM SUMMARY

Psalm 23 is a personal affirmation of faith. It is timeless—so simple a child can understand it, yet so profound no interpreter has ever captured its full meaning. God is likened to a shepherd. The psalm looks at a number of tasks of a shepherd and shows how these tasks reveal what God does for us.

God's Provision (23:1–6)

PROVISION	VERSE	PASSAGE
Rest	2	"He makes me lie down in green pastures"
Life	3	"He restores my soul"
Guidance	3	"He guides me in paths of righteousness"
Safety	4	"I will fear no evil, for you are with me"
Provision for flock	5	"My cup overflows"
Heavenly home	6	"I will dwell in the house of the LORD forever"

Note also that the psalm begins by referring to God in the third person ("the LORD [he] is my shepherd"). Then there is a shift to usage of the second person ("you are with me," v. 4). We use the second person only to speak of someone who is present.

According to Oriental custom, the host would guarantee the safety of the psalmist, even in the presence of his enemies.

■ *The psalmist gives a personal affirmation of*
■ *faith. The Lord is his Shepherd. In this way,*
■ *he views God as his provider, guide, com-*
■ *forter, and protector.*

GUIDING QUESTION

Jesus obviously knew and loved this psalm. Christians through the centuries have cherished this psalm. What does Psalm 23 mean to you?

PSALM 24: NATURE, MAN, AND GOD

Theme: A hymn to the King of glory

Reader insights: A processional hymn, and a portrayal of Israel's worship. This is a messianic psalm, as it prophesys about the Messiah to come.

PSALM SUMMARY

Nature: The world about us (24:1–2). The psalm opens with a ringing affirmation of the Lord's ownership of the world.

Man: The world within (24:3–6). It then raises the question of who may come into the Lord's presence on His holy mountain. Priests answer from within the Temple area. These verses describe the kind of person who may pay homage to the King. The worshiper should be a person of integrity. He is to be pure in hand and heart; in action and intention. Both his motives and his deeds are to be right. He is to be neither proud nor deceitful (v. 4).

God: The world beyond (24:7–10). Verses 7–10 describe the entrance of the King into Jerusalem. The choir with the procession poetically addresses the Temple gates (v. 7). Voices of priests from within ask, "Who is this King of glory?" The choir replies that He is "the LORD mighty in battle" (a warrior God); and He is "the

Background: Pilgrims coming to the city of Jerusalem for a festival would march in procession. After coming around the Mount of Olives and crossing the Kidron Valley, the procession would halt at the gate to the Temple courtyard. This psalm was sung antiphonally with the choir outside asking, "Who is this King of glory?" The priests within would reply, "The Lord Almighty, He is the King of glory."

Lord of hosts" (armies). This is a poetic way of speaking of the Lord as a God of might and great power. Israel felt that the Lord led their armies to victory in battle. This term, "the LORD Almighty," occurs more than 250 times in the Old Testament.

Lessons in living: The earth is God's. All belongs to Him; we are only stewards of what He gives us. Let us pay homage to the King, for He is in control of all we have.

Background: Psalm 25 is an acrostic. Each verse begins with a different letter of the Hebrew alphabet, of which there are twenty-two. Because of this, its thought does not flow smoothly. The verses alternate between prayers and expressions of the psalmist's confidence in God.

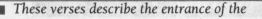

■ *These verses describe the entrance of the*
■ *King into Jerusalem. Here the choir with the*
■ *procession poetically addresses the Temple*
■ *gates and dialogues with the priests within.*
■ *The proclamation that rings out is that He is*
■ *"the King of glory!"*

GUIDING QUESTION

What three "worlds" does the psalmist celebrate?

PSALM 25: A PRAYER OF TRUST AND LAMENT

Theme: Trust in God, a plea for divine guidance, and prayer for forgiveness

Reader insights: This psalm was likely a literary composition. Later, it may have been used in communal worship.

PSALM SUMMARY

Prayer for protection, guidance, and pardon (25:1–7). The psalm begins with the writer's assertion of trust in God (vv. 1–2). Repeatedly, he asks that he not be "put to shame" in the presence of his enemies. The psalmist prays for the Lord's guidance and leading (vv. 4–5). He asks that God remember his mercy and *not* remember his sins

(vv. 6–7). Two words are used for his wrongdoing: "sins and transgressions."

God's goodness, fairness, and faithfulness (25:8–15). The covenant character of God dominates the psalmist's expression of confidence. God is upright and instructs sinners in the right way to live (v. 8). His steadfast love causes Him to keep His covenant with His chosen ones (vv. 9–10). God acts with justice. The psalmist renews his prayer to be forgiven (v. 11). He longs to enjoy friendship with the Lord (vv. 12–15).

Prayers for deliverance (25:16–21). In his loneliness, the psalmist asks for divine grace (vv. 15–16). The word translated "forgive" means "to lift a burden"—an apt description of guilt and forgiveness. The final verse is a prayer for the nation. It has been appended to the personal prayer that makes up the body of the psalm. This made it more useful in public worship.

■ *The psalmist asks for divine grace so he may*
■ *be delivered from his anguish.*

GUIDING QUESTION
Upon what does the psalmist base his confidence in verses 8–15?

PSALM 26: VINDICATE THE INNOCENT

Background: The psalmist has been accused of wrongdoing. He protests that he is innocent and goes to the Temple, seeking vindication (see 1 Kings 8:31–32). He does not claim to be sinless, but declares himself innocent of the charges brought against him. He appeals for justice based on his integrity.

Theme: Preparation for entering the Temple
Reader insights: A song of trust. This psalm is similar to Psalms 7 and 17 and is a companion to Psalm 28.

PSALM SUMMARY

A plea for vindication (26:1–3). The psalmist has been loyal to God, with a lifestyle of personal integrity. A person of integrity is one whose speech and actions are congruent. His faith and trust in God are unshaken; therefore, he can pray for justice. He asks that God would prove, try, and test him in heart and mind.

A plea of innocence (26:4–7). The worshiper insists that he has refrained from running with the wrong crowd. He does not consort with the wicked (vv. 4–5). In a ritual to symbolize his innocence, he washes his hands before the Lord (v. 6). This is what Pilate did following the trial of Jesus (Matt. 27:24). Ritual washing of one's hands before worship was customary as a symbol of purity (Exod. 30:17–21). Next, he goes around the altar with a procession, singing about God's mighty acts (vv. 6–7).

A plea of devotion (26:8–12). The psalmist loves God's house where God's glory dwells (v. 8). God's glory is His revealed presence symbolized by the ark and mercy seat (Exod. 33:18–22). The psalmist is comfortable with God and can trust Him to judge fairly. He asks to be spared the fate of the wicked, including premature death (vv. 9–10). He feels secure, "on level ground," before the Lord (v. 12). This means that he will continue to walk in his integrity, believing that dangerous obstacles in his path will be removed.

- **■ *The psalmist is convinced that he can trust***
- **■ *God to judge him fairly. He feels secure and***
- **■ *attests to his faith.***

GUIDING QUESTION

What evidence do we have of the psalmist's devotion to God?

PSALM 27: CONQUERING FEAR

Theme: Trust in God

Reader insights: A song of trust. There are two distinct moods reflected here. The first six verses constitute an affirmation of faith. Verses 7–14 are a lament and prayer for help. Both reflect the psalmist's trust in God.

PSALM SUMMARY

The psalmist declares his faith (27:1–3). No one is immune from fear. The psalmist trusts in the Lord and discovers that he need have no ultimate fear (v. 1). He uses three military metaphors to express his trust: God is his light, his salvation, his stronghold.

The psalmist describes his life with the Lord (27:4–12). The psalmist's great desire is the privilege of worship in God's house (cp. v. 4 with Ps. 23:6). He enjoys worship and feels secure in the divine presence. He also finds guidance when he would "seek him in his temple" (v. 4). God

Background: This psalm dates back to the beginning of Saul's persecution of David. Later, and until the present century, Psalm 27 has played a central role in *Yamin Noraim* ("Days of Awe"), being recited in the synagogue during each of the ten holy days.

protects those who trust in Him (v. 5). They bring their offering of gratitude and sing God's praise with "shouts of joy" (v. 6). Beginning with verse 7, the psalmist begins his plea to have his prayer heard. This passage is a study in the anatomy of prayer.

The psalm ends on a note of quiet confidence. The psalmist is not overcome by his fears but trusts in the goodness of the Lord. He expects to see God's goodness in his own lifetime (v. 13). He will see the guidance and protection he seeks from God.

The closing verse of the psalm is a great admonition based on solid religious experience. They are the words of the king to a priest or temple servant, but this admonition is for every believer in every age: "Wait for the LORD; be strong and take heart and wait for the LORD."

■ *In these final two verses, the psalm ends on a*
■ *note of quiet confidence. The psalmist is not*
■ *overcome by his fears but rather trusts in the*
■ *goodness of the Lord. He fully expects to see*
■ *the guidance and protection he seeks from*
■ *God.*

GUIDING QUESTION
In verse 1 the psalmist uses three military metaphors to express his trust. What are they and what does each mean?

PSALM 28: A CRY FOR HELP

Theme: Hope is in God alone

Reader insights: A song of trust. Here we have a personal lament which turns into an answered prayer. It is a companion to Psalm 26, which is a prayer for justice, while Psalm 28 is an appeal for mercy. Both psalms plead for deliverance, focusing on the Temple as a symbol of God's saving presence.

Background: This psalm was likely part of a liturgy of supplication conducted in the Temple. We do not know whether such a ritual would be conducted in a time of need or if it was conducted at one of the annual festivals.

PSALM SUMMARY

A cry for help (28:1–5). The psalmist feels keenly the absence of God. He makes an appeal to be heard by God. The *pit* in verse 1 is a synonym for Sheol, the abode of the dead.

He lifts up his hands in prayer, facing the holy of holies in the Temple, where God is present (v. 2). The characteristic stance for prayer among the Hebrews was standing, lifting one's hands, palms up, toward heaven. Our present-day common stance—kneeling, bowing, and folding one's hands in prayer—dates from medieval times.

The psalmist prays that God's law might prevail, giving the wicked what they deserve (vv. 4–5). He asks that he be spared their fate (v. 3).

Answered prayer (28:6–7). We see a dramatic change in the mood at verse 6. The author feels that God begins to hear and answer his prayer. His plea gives way to adoration and expression of his faith and gratitude.

Prayer for the nation (28:8–9). Now the psalm's focus shifts from the psalmist to the nation. God is the "strength" and "fortress" of His people (v. 8). The last verse is a series of short petitions.

■ *The psalm closes with a shift in focus from*
■ *the psalmist to the nation. Here the psalmist*
■ *declares that God is the "strength" and "for-*
■ *tress" of His people.*

GUIDING QUESTIONS

What pattern do we see in the psalmist's prayer in verses 8–9? How might we follow this model today?

PSALM 29: THE VOICE OF GOD IN NATURE

Background: Israel is a dry land where it does not rain for months each year. Then in the autumn, clouds come in from the Mediterranean Sea, bringing welcome rain. This psalm could have been used in worship, celebrating the return of these life-giving rainstorms.

Theme: The glory of God revealed in nature
Reader insights: A hymn. This psalm is one of the most majestic and dramatic poems in the Psalter.

PSALM SUMMARY

Let the angels join in worship (29:1–2). In Psalms 8 and 19 the authors were aware of the presence of God in nature—in the calm night sky. This psalmist experienced God in the fury of a thunderstorm. The psalmist summons the angelic host surrounding God's throne to join in worship. They are called to ascribe glory to God, while human worshipers did the same in His Temple on earth. Heaven and earth unite in His praise.

The voice of God in the storm (29:3–9). Seven times the writer states: "The voice of the LORD," suggesting seven peals of thunder (see Ps. 18:13; Job 37:2–5; Rev. 10:3). The psalmist notes the dramatic effects of the fierce storm (v. 3–9). His people respond by crying, "Glory!"

The calm after the storm (29:10–11). God is in control of the flood and the storm. (The Hebrew word used here for *flood* is also used in Gen. 6:11 of Noah's flood.) Ancient pagans, such as the Babylonians, thought the gods themselves were frightened and threatened by the flood. Therefore, God could give His people strength and peace because He controls the rainstorms. The storm is glorious to the people because it demonstrates God's power and His provision of rain. We, too, are equally dependent on God and can see His power and beauty in nature—whether it be calm or fierce.

- *God is in control of the flood and the storm.*
- *To God's people, the storm is glorious*
- *because it demonstrates God's power and His*
- *provision of rain.*

GUIDING QUESTION
How did God use the storm to reveal Himself?

PSALM 30: JOY IN THE MORNING

Theme: Praise to the Lord for His lovingkindness
Reader insights: This is a hymn of thanksgiving for healing. The writer uses many contrasts as a means of engaging his readers and encouraging them.

Background: This psalm was used in a ceremony of thanksgiving, likely held in the Temple. We know it was used in public worship, for it asks that other believers join in praise to God (v. 4).

PSALM SUMMARY

The psalmist's thanksgiving (30:1–4). The psalmist is critically ill (v. 2), and his death would have pleased his enemies (v. 1). In his distress he cries out to God. The Almighty hears his prayer and heals him. Drawing him up from the verge of death, God restores his health (v. 3). The word for "lifted me up" is the same word the Hebrews used for pulling a bucket up from the well. Here, the psalmist has been drawn up from the pit of death by God's divine hand. As a result of His help, the psalmist praises the Lord and invites others to join him in thanksgiving (v. 4).

God defeats the psalmist's enemies, answers his prayer, saves his life, gives him stability, and gives him joy. The psalmist's humble attitude is an example for all believers.

From weeping to rejoicing (30:5). The psalmist considers his suffering a sign of God's "anger," due to his own sin. He is confident, however, that the divine displeasure will be temporary, to be replaced by God's favor, which will last throughout his lifetime. Then he contrasts tears and joy. He cries through the night of suffering. But "rejoicing comes in the morning." The psalmist contrasts the night of crying with the morning's joy. Weeping is temporary, but joy is enduring.

The psalmist's testimony (30:6–12). Prior to his illness the psalmist had enjoyed prosperity and felt both secure and self-sufficient (v. 6). It is easy to feel quite confident as long as everything is going well. We may even be tempted to feel cocky and proud, thinking that we deserve our good health and affluence—that having them is our right.

Everything suddenly changes for the psalmist (vv. 7–9). In his illness, God seems far away. He is at the point of panic and begins to pray earnestly (vv. 7–8). He tries to reason with the

Lord, thinking that he may able to strike a bargain with the Almighty (v. 9).

After all, if he dies and returns to dust, he can no longer serve and praise the Lord.

We see his prayer taking on a new dimension at verse 10. He prays in complete reliance on God's grace—not on the basis of what he feels he deserves.

At that point, God hears him and grants his request for healing and help. In happy response he declares that God had turned his somber sackcloth of sorrow into bright garments of gladness. He goes from mourning to joy (vv. 11–12). In his exultation he promises to give God "thanks forever."

In the course of his experience, the psalmist strengthens his faith and his understanding of God. He moves from an attitude of self-sufficiency (v. 6), to bargaining with God (v. 9), to utter dependence on God's grace (v. 10). This is a normal progression we often see in a maturing religious experience. Note that the psalmist does not fail to give thanks for his deliverance.

- *In the course of his experience, the psalmist*
- *strengthens his faith and his understanding*
- *of God. He moves from an attitude of*
- *self-sufficiency to utter dependence on God's*
- *grace.*

GUIDING QUESTIONS

What is the psalmist's attitude toward life? What becomes his predicament? What can we as believers today learn from his experience?

PSALM 31: INTO GOD'S HANDS

Background: The background of this psalm is thought to be the Desert of Maon, when David was being pursued by Saul (1 Sam. 23).

Theme: The psalmist's trust in God and the fulfillment of that trust

Reader insights: An individual lament. The structure of this psalm alternates between lament and thanksgiving, between a plea for help and praise of God's goodness. Some have thought it the blending of two different psalms. More likely, it is simply an expression of the tension between times of trouble and trust in God.

PSALM SUMMARY

A cry for deliverance (31:1–8). The psalmist begins with a testimony of his trust in God. God had been his refuge in past times of trouble (v. 1). He asks God to be his mountain fortress now and in the future (v. 2). The Judean hill country was a place of safety in a time of invasion or similar danger. This psalm brings to mind David fleeing King Saul in that region. The psalmist's enemies were out to trap him as a hunter ensnares an animal (v. 4). This theme is often repeated in the Psalms (see 9:15; 35:7; 57:6; 140:5). His expressions of his needs are quite elaborate. They include: danger in battle, illness, loneliness, threat, persecution, and ensnaring enemies.

"Into your hand I commit my spirit" was the psalmist's prayer of trust in the presence of his enemies (v. 5). How appropriate that Jesus' last words from the cross were this prayer of faith. The psalmist adds his personal address, "Father" (Luke 23:46).

Verse 7 is a further statement of the psalmist's confidence in God's trustworthy love. Though his enemies have him in a tight (narrow) place, he believes God will set his feet "in a spacious place" (v. 8).

"Spacious place"

These words are just one word in the Hebrew text. The word means "broad, roomy place." Setting one's feet in a spacious place is a figure of speech signifying freedom from distress and anxiety.

A lament (31:9–18). The psalmist next describes his "distress" in greater detail. He is depressed and filled with grief (vv. 9–10). He suffers the scorn of his enemies (v. 11) and feels as forgotten as the dead. He is as useless as a broken clay pot (v. 12). His enemies carry out a campaign of whispers against him, plotting to kill him (v. 13).

Even in this plight, the psalmist's trust in God is not shaken: "You are my God" (v. 14) and "My times are in your hands" (v. 15). God is in control of his destiny. These are powerful affirmations of faith. He prays that he might not be put to shame, but that his enemies will (v. 17).

A thanksgiving (31:19–24). Divine goodness is not stingy but "abundant" (cp. Ps. 23:5). This favor and protection is available to all who trust in the Lord (vv. 19–20). Finally, the psalmist calls on all believers to "love the LORD . . . be strong and take heart . . . hope (depend) in the LORD" (vv. 23–24).

■ *The psalmist describes his distress in great*
■ *detail. Despite his grief and depression, he*
■ *reaffirms his trust in God.*

GUIDING QUESTION

The psalmist affirms that "my times are in your hands." What does this mean to the believer today?

PSALM 32: THE JOY OF FORGIVENESS

Background: Many scholars associate this psalm with David's sin with Bathsheba.

Theme: God's blessing of forgiveness

Reader insights: A song of testimony. This is the second of the penitential psalms used in Christian worship (Pss. 6; 32; 38; 51; 102; 130; 143). Psalm 32 is also a song of thanksgiving and a wisdom poem. It was the favorite psalm of Augustine, who placed a copy of it on the wall beside his bed.

PSALM SUMMARY

The joy of forgiveness (32:1–2). This psalm begins with a beatitude, "Blessed is he whose transgressions are forgiven, whose sins are covered" (v. 1).

The burden of guilt (32:3–4). Here David recalls his experience. There had been a time when he refused to acknowledge his sin (v. 3). The resulting guilt becomes an unbearable burden. It makes him literally ill and depressed. He comes under conviction for his sins—"Your hand was heavy upon me" (v. 4). He feels this burden "day and night," a figure of speech indicating a continuous and unceasing burden. A guilty conscience can have dire consequences, both physically and emotionally.

Sin confessed and forgiven (32:5). David now acknowledges his sin. The tense of the Hebrew verb is literally "*I began to acknowledge*," and suggests that this is the first step toward securing pardon. Once David freely acknowledges his sin, he experiences divine forgiveness. Of course, God already knew about his sin. Confession means that the psalmist decides to give up his self-deceit. To his great relief, God lifts his burden of guilt and gives his song back.

The three words for sin in verses 1–2 are matched by a second set of three terms describing what God does with our sin. The psalmist uses three equally powerful words to describe divine forgiveness:

1. His sins are "forgiven" or literally lifted as a burden from the shoulders—they were "rolled away."
2. His crimes are "covered" by the divine Judge—"case dismissed."
3. "The LORD does not count against him."

A witness from experience (32:6–9). He calls on others to pray also when they find themselves in distress (v. 6), and then praises God for protecting and guarding him (v. 7).

A call to rejoice (32:10–11). The writer contrasts the lot of the wicked with that of the righteous, who are surrounded by steadfast love (v. 10). Grace envelops those who trust God. In the final verse he sounds a threefold call to joy: "Rejoice . . . be glad . . . sing!"

■ *The psalmist gives a testimony of his experi-*
■ *ence. He instructs others in the right way,*
■ *contrasting the wicked with that of the righ-*
■ *teous. He closes with a threefold call to joy.*

Three Words for *Sin*

Transgression (Heb., *peshah*). This word literally means "departure." In this case, it has the sense of rebellion against God and His authority. It is deliberate disobedience of God's will, and describes sin in view of our relationship to God.

Sin (Heb., *chattath*). This word is translated "sin" in verse 1. It is a nearly exact equivalent of the New Testament word for *sin.* Both mean "falling short" of the mark. In the ancient world this was an archery term describing a person who shoots at a target but whose arrow falls short. It signifies moral failure, and describes sin in relation to the divine law.

Iniquity (Heb., *hawon*). This word is also translated by the NIV as "sin" (v. 2). It means "corrupt," "twisted," or "crooked." It signifies crooked and perverse qualities, and describes sin in relation to ourselves.

GUIDING QUESTION

The psalmist uses three different words for *sin*. Combining the unique meanings of each, what do we learn about sin?

PSALM 33: GOD'S WORK AND WORD

Theme: Praise and thanks to God for His Word and works

Reader insights: A hymn of praise, and one of the few psalms without a title. It contains many of the basic themes of Hebrew theology, such as the creation, the covenant, and the human response of worship. The structure of this psalm expresses many of those aspects of worship such as adoration, celebration, and dedication.

Background: The setting of this psalm is the congregation at worship.

PSALM SUMMARY

Call to worship (33:1–3). The writer invites the faithful to praise the Lord with the lyre and harp. These are representative musical instruments that were used to accompany congregational singing. We find a more complete list of ancient musical instruments used in worship in Psalm 150.

God's creative Word (33:4–9). The psalmist focuses on God's attributes and characterizes the divine activity as truthful, faithful, righteous, and just (vv. 4–5). The Lord created the heavens by His word (v. 6). In verse 4 we see that His "word" and "work" are parallel.

God's creative power inspires reverence and awe. His power is such that He appears to create effortlessly.

METAPHOR	POINT
"By the word of the LORD were the heavens made"	The creative power of God's word
"He gathers the waters . . . into jars"	The greatness of God against the smallness of the world

God's plan and purpose (33:10–12). God not only made the world, but He also continues to care about it. He is involved with His creation and His creatures. Here we have a clear contrast between the counsel of God and the thoughts of the people. The plans of the nations don't amount to much, but the purpose of God determines the outcome of history (vv. 10–11). In verse 12 we have a ringing beatitude and benediction: "Blessed is the nation whose God is the LORD."

God's providential care (33:13–19). God watches over people. He is not detached and disinterested like the Greek gods. He observes people's actions and knows what is in their hearts (their intentions). The Almighty is at work in history as surely as He was at work in creation. "The eyes of the LORD" in verse 18 is a way of speaking of divine providence. The destiny of people and nations is in His hands. Believers are under His watchful care (vv. 18–19).

Sovereign God, our basis of hope (33:20–22). The psalm begins with joyous praise; it ends with a note of joyous trust. It calls the reader to three actions:

1. Patient dependence on the Lord (v. 20);
2. "Trust in his holy name" (v. 21); and
3. "Hope" in the Lord, due to His "unfailing love" (v. 22).

This closing prayer serves to summarize the message of the psalm.

■ *The writer focuses on God's attributes and*
■ *describes God's creative power. It is the*
■ *power of the Almighty that commands our*
■ *awe and reverence. God observes the activi-*
■ *ties of His people, watching over them and*
■ *caring for their needs.*

GUIDING QUESTION

What does the statement "the eyes of the LORD are on those who fear him" (v. 18) mean?

PSALM 34: TASTE AND SEE THAT THE LORD IS GOOD

Background: The title of this psalm alludes to events described in 1 Samuel 21:10-15. It is the account of David feigning insanity before Achish, king of Gath.

Theme: Encouragement to praise and trust God

Reader insights: A song of testimony. This is a companion psalm to Psalm 25. Both are acrostics, which means that each verse begins with the succeeding letter of the Hebrew alphabet, of which there are twenty-two. Psalm 25 is a lament, whereas Psalm 34 is a thanksgiving and an invitation to try faith in God. They are both what is called *wisdom literature* and have a teaching purpose.

PSALM SUMMARY

Invitation to gratitude (34:1-7). The psalmist praises the Lord and invites other worshipers to join in his joy. "Glorify the LORD with me; let us exalt his name together" (v. 3). He then boasts about the faithfulness of God (cp. 1 Cor. 1:31).

The Lord "delivered" the psalmist from fear, trouble, and affliction (vv. 4, 17, 19). The word literally means the Lord "snatched" him from danger at the last moment. Therefore, instead of his blushing with shame, his face was radiant, glowing at his fellowship with the Lord (v. 5). The poor and oppressed are saved by the Lord (v. 6). And the "angel of the LORD" protects those who have reverence (fear) for God (v. 7). The angel of the Lord is His messenger who represents the Lord Himself (see Exod. 23:20; Judg. 6:11–23).

Invitation to experience (34:8–11). The psalmist invites others to try God for themselves—to taste and see—to have a firsthand relationship with Him.

The "fear of the Lord" is an Old Testament way of describing reverence (v. 9). "Saints" are believers. God provides for them (v. 10). In this part of the psalm the poet took the role of a teacher instructing his students, "my children" (v. 11), on the theme of reverence. This passage is similar to Proverbs 1–9. Reverence is intended to issue in ethical conduct.

Fulfillment of life (34:12–14). Verse 12 is a summary of reverence. Those who want to live long should refrain from speaking deceitfully, turn from wrong and do what is right, and seek those things that lead to peace. At this point, the psalmist issues a series of imperatives to challenge his readers to these ends. First Peter 3:10–12 quotes verses 12–16 from this psalm.

The justice and nearness of God (34:15–22). The psalmist uses vivid metaphors of God in verses

"Glorify the LORD"

The word translated "glorify" is the word that means "magnify" or "make great." To magnify God is to bring our own poor sense of Him more in line with His majestic reality.

15–16: "The eyes of the LORD . . . his ears . . . the face of the LORD." The psalmist teaches that the Lord cares for the righteous but cuts off the remembrance of the wicked. He is the deliverer of the righteous (vv. 17, 19). Evil contains the seed of its own destruction (v. 21). But God redeems and forgives those who trust in Him (v. 22). "No one will be condemned who takes refuge in him." He ransoms His own, paying their sin debt. This, of course, is possible because of the death and resurrection of Jesus Christ.

- *The psalmist contrasts the estates of the righ-*
- *teous and the wicked. God's ultimate deliver-*
- *ance is from the eternal punishment of sin,*
- *which is by the death and resurrection of*
- *Jesus Christ.*

GUIDING QUESTIONS
For what is the psalmist grateful? What does it mean to "glorify" or "magnify" the Lord?

PSALM 35: TROUBLE COMES IN THREES

Theme: Praise for deliverance from the danger of death

Reader insights: An individual lament. An old saying has it that "trouble comes in threes." The author of Psalm 35 might well agree. It is a threefold lament. Each plea for deliverance concludes with a brief thanksgiving for divine help (vv. 10, 18, 28).

PSALM SUMMARY

"Contend, O LORD" (35:1–10). The first of three laments is "Contend, O LORD" (1–10). Here we have the vivid poetic imagery of battle. We see a picture of the Lord fighting on behalf of the psalmist. His enemies are God's enemies (v. 1). He asks that they be put to shame, be confounded, and be driven before the angel of the Lord like chaff before the wind (vv. 4–5; cp. Ps. 1:4). Comparing an enemy to chaff is a graphic picture of the complete rout of that enemy. Without provocation the psalmist's enemies had set nets and dug a pit to ensnare him. He asks that they fall prey to their own traps (vv. 7–8).

The psalmist vows to rejoice and praise God for His deliverance. "Who is like you, O LORD?" is a phrase of adoration. This statement causes the reader to consider the uniqueness of God. He alone is Creator, sustainer, and our heavenly Father. There is no one else in the universe who has His limitless power and love.

"O LORD, how long" (35:11–18). The reason for the second lament, "O LORD, how long" (11–18), is that "ruthless witnesses" attack the

Background: Some commentators believe that Psalm 35 is a composite of three different psalms. It is similar to Psalm 7. The enemies here may be personal, or they may be rival nations who challenge the king's authority. The poem is a cry for vindication. It is highly emotional, expressing both hurt and anger. The poet is convinced both of his own innocence and of God's power to set the record straight.

psalmist's reputation. They fabricate lies and falsely accuse him of crimes. The irony of the situation is not their wickedness as much as their *ingratitude.* When they were ill, he had done everything possible to help them. He wore sackcloth and fasted. He grieved and prayed for them as one would for a brother or his own mother (vv. 13–14).

Yet, when the psalmist became ill or found himself in trouble, these same persons "gathered in glee." They slandered and mocked him. Ingratitude from those we have helped is a bitter pill to swallow. We should help others without expecting to be thanked, but we should always remember to be grateful to all who help us. In exasperation, the psalmist cries out, "O LORD, how long?" and pleas for rescue (v. 17). In the final verse of this section the refrain of praise appears again (v. 18).

"Vindicate me . . . O LORD" (35:19–28). A third time the psalmist laments his enemies, crying out, "Vindicate me . . . O LORD" (19–28). They wink at one another knowingly and hate him without reason (v. 19). They are not men of peace like "those who live quietly in the land" (v. 20).

Rather, they are contemptuous and deceitful. Like children, they make fun of him, saying, "Aha! Aha!" (v. 21). The psalmist prays for God to come to his aid—to vindicate him in the sight of his enemies (vv. 22–24). He wants them discredited (v. 26).The psalm concludes with its third refrain of praise (v. 28). The psalmist reminds us that people can be vicious and ungrateful. However, the three prayers of praise at the conclusion of each stanza show his faith that God will provide a solution to his dilemma (see Ps. 4). This kind of faith was beautifully exemplified by Jesus in the Garden of Gethsemane (Matt. 26:36–46).

■ *The psalmist delivers three laments regard-*
■ *ing his enemies. The psalmist prays for God*
■ *to come to his aid and vindicate him in the*
■ *sight of his enemies. He concludes with a*
■ *refrain of praise.*

GUIDING QUESTIONS

What is the theme of this psalm? How is it structured for the reader?

PSALM 36: WICKEDNESS OF MAN—GOODNESS OF GOD

Theme: The way of the wicked and the loving-kindness of God
Reader insight: A song of testimony.

PSALM SUMMARY

The way of the wicked (36:1–4). The psalmist personifies evil here as a demonic spirit. It "whispers" to the heart of the wicked, telling them they have nothing to fear from God. Satan is the "father of lies." Paul quoted the last half of the first verse in his description of human depravity (Rom. 3:18). The ungodly person asks, "Who is to know?" He thinks God will not care or find out what he is up to (v. 2).

The wicked flatter themselves to make themselves look good in their own eyes. They hate to

Background: The wickedness of man is used as a foil for the goodness of God in this psalm. The psalmist contrasts the character of God with the sinfulness of man. In the title David is called "the servant of the LORD" (see 1 Sam. 23:10–11).

admit they are wrong. They easily rationalize their evil, at least for a time. They live like blindfolded people in a world of illusion. Their mouths are filled with deceit (v. 3) and their lives with mischief rather than good (v. 4). The end result is self-deception.

The lovingkindness of God (36:5–9). Against the backdrop of humanity's evil desires and actions, the psalmist sings of God's righteousness. The worshiper is reminded of several of God's characteristic traits: steadfast love, righteousness, protection, and provision. God provides many delightful things for our well-being. God is the source of our life (Jer. 2:13) and our light (John 1:14).

The Hebrew word for "delights" is *Eden,* with its river and garden paradise (Gen. 2:10). Compare Jeremiah 2:13 on the fountain of life (v. 9).

A closing prayer (36:10–12). In this concluding prayer the psalmist asks for God's continued steadfast love and His salvation from the wickedness of others. Note the vivid figures, "the foot of the proud" and "the hand of the wicked" (v. 11). To "know" the Lord (v. 10) means to commit oneself to Him and to live in faithful relationship with Him (see Isa. 1:14).

■ *The psalmist sings of God's righteousness,*
■ *focusing on steadfast love, righteousness,*
■ *protection, and provision. The psalmist con-*
■ *cludes by asking God for His continued*
■ *steadfast love and His salvation from the*
■ *wickedness of others.*

GUIDING QUESTION

How does the psalmist characterize the way of the wicked?

PSALM 37: WISDOM IN CAPSULE FORM

Theme: The problem of evil

Reader insights: A wisdom song. This poem is a collection of wise sayings by an elder to his students. It is in the form of an acrostic—every other line begins with the succeeding letter of the Hebrew alphabet. Here we find the traditional theology of the Old Testament: the righteous prosper, and the wicked suffer. Its corollary is that suffering is due to sin. This psalm should be read in connection with Psalm 73 and the book of Job. We see in the Old Testament how severely Job questioned that point of view.

Background: The psalm is made up of a group of twenty proverbs. Suffering is often the result of sin, but not always. The affliction of the godly posed a real problem for Old Testament people, as it does for modern-day believers. Their difficulty was greater than ours, however, because they had no clear idea of life after death with opportunity for reward and punishment.

PSALM SUMMARY

"Do not fret" (37:1–11). The wise teacher begins by instructing his pupils not to be upset by or jealous of the prosperity of the wicked. He insists that the success of the wicked will be temporary (v. 10). Taking the long view, the meek shall ultimately possess the land (v. 11; see Matt. 5:5).

"The LORD laughs at the wicked" (37:12–22). The time of recompense for the wicked is certain: "Their day is coming" (v. 13). They may plot to destroy the righteous, but their weapons will recoil on them (vv. 14–15). The little that the righteous enjoy is better than the plenty of the wicked (vv. 16–17). High-handed prosperity, a quick profit, and too-easy credit will not long succeed (vv. 18–19). By contrast, the righteous are generous (v. 21). But the wicked will "vanish like smoke" (v. 20). They are doomed to perish.

God directs the steps of the righteous (37:23–33). "The LORD delights in a man's way, he makes his steps firm" (v. 23). The righteous are not left to their own wisdom. Even if they fall, they will get up again. The experienced psalmist has never seen the righteous forsaken or his children begging (vv. 25–26). While there may be exceptions, this is remarkably true today as well.

"Wait for the LORD" (37:34–40). The wise teacher recommends patience. Those who trust in the Lord find that He helps them, delivers them, and saves them (v. 40). God takes care of His own. Waiting for the Lord constitutes an act of faith. To wait patiently on the Lord often is not easy. Like Job, we need to learn that it is more important to trust God than to have answers to all our questions.

■ *Rather than actively combat the wicked, the*
■ *wise teacher recommends patience. It is God*
■ *who helps and saves His people.*

GUIDING QUESTION
What counsel does the wise teacher give for dealing with the prosperity of the wicked?

Psalm 38: Sin and Suffering

Theme: Request for mercy and help from God for sickness

Reader insights: An individual lament. The theology of Psalm 37 is expanded here. The poet is convinced that his dreadful suffering is punishment for his sin. The psalm's vivid description of suffering caused the church to make use of it during Holy Week worship. Its theme is similar to the experiences of Job, Jeremiah, and Jesus.

Background: This psalm was intended to be primarily a literary composition for use in the devotional life of the sick or afflicted person.

PSALM SUMMARY

Physical illness (38:1–10). The psalmist mentions his physical agony fifteen times in this psalm. He considers it a punishment from God for his sins. Repenting, he asks for divine mercy.

The opening of the psalm is very similar to that of Psalm 6. He does not expect to escape punishment for his sin but asks that it be tempered (vv. 1–2). In vivid terms he describes his agony of body and soul. His heart throbs; his strength drains away; and his eyes grow dim (v. 10).

Rejected and oppressed (38:11–20). The people he thought he could count on are keeping their distance. They are afraid of being defiled or catching his disease (see Lev. 13:45–56). He is an untouchable, ostracized by those dearest to him. The psalmist does not rebuke them, but instead looks to the Lord for help (vv. 13–15).

The psalmist's enemies boast and rejoice at his misfortune (v. 16). His enemies are numerous and vigorous in their activity, and he does not deserve their enmity (vv. 19–20). But the psalmist confesses his sin to God, casting himself on God's mercy (v. 18).

An appeal for God's help (38:21–22). In his utter helplessness the psalmist acknowledges his reliance on God. His poem begins and ends with an appeal to God (see Ps. 22:1). Despite his sin, the psalmist trusts God to answer his prayer. We can be sure that his prayer was heard, for the sinner's prayer of repentance always is.

This psalm depicts profound suffering, the confession of sin, and a prayer for salvation. While not all suffering is due to sin, still, when trouble comes, we inevitably ask *why*.

- ■ *The psalmist acknowledges his reliance on*
- ■ *God and trusts God to answer him, despite*
- ■ *his sin.*

GUIDING QUESTION
What are some of the key themes of this psalm?

Background: This psalm portrays the despair of one about to die, with no hope of life afterward. It contains a conversation between the poet and God. He candidly asks the meaning of mankind's brief life and the mystery of death. He tries to be silent (vv. 1–3) but finally has to speak up.

PSALM 39: A DESPERATE PRAYER

Theme: The problem of sin and suffering

Reader insights: An individual lament. What are we to make of death? The ancient Israelites had no clear word from God about life after death. Their only idea of immortality seems to have been that a person lives on through his children. "Sheol" was the mysterious abode of the dead—a shadowy land of nothingness, a waste. The real hope and promise of eternal life was accomplished through the resurrection of Jesus Christ.

The psalmist keeps quiet (39:1–3). The psalmist holds his peace in the presence of the wicked. He muzzles his mouth and does not ask the ultimate questions burning within him. But his silence does not help as his pain grows worse; his agony increases.

The psalmist speaks out (39:4–6). He now cries out in anguish. All human effort appears futile. He cannot cure himself and keep death at bay. Life is brief and fleeting at best—only a few "handbreadths" (the width of four fingers). Human life is fragile—a mere breath (vv. 5, 11). Even a short life is filled with trouble and turmoil. Here the psalmist sounds like the writer of Ecclesiastes. Man's life is no more than a fleeting shadow (v. 6).

All that is left is faith (39:7–11). What awaits after death? The psalmist does not know the answer, but he does know "my hope is in you" (v. 7). He prays for divine forgiveness before he dies (v. 8). Faith and repentance are his way of seeking relief. He feels that his serious illness is punishment for his sin (as in Ps. 38). The problem is that this punishment is consuming him "like a moth" (v. 11) eating clothes.

A prayer of desperation (39:12–13). With beautiful poetry the psalmist prays for God to hear him. He confesses that he is merely a pilgrim, a passing guest on the earth, an "alien, a stranger" (v. 12). But if God's punishment is not soon lifted, he will pass away completely! (v. 13).

The prayer and psalm end abruptly, and not on a note of bright hope: "Hear my prayer, O LORD, listen to my cry for help . . . that I may rejoice again" (vv. 12, 13). There is no indication that his prayer was heard and answered. While no assurance is given, the one positive note here is the psalmist's enduring faith. How much brighter should be our faith when we have the hope of glory! This psalm should make us appreciate the gospel of our risen Lord even more.

- ■ *The psalmist closes with a desperate prayer*
- ■ *that soon turns to hope. While we do not*
- ■ *know whether the prayer was answered, we*
- ■ *do see the psalmist's faith.*

GUIDING QUESTION

What is the basis of the psalmist's hope in verses 12–13?

PSALM 40: A TESTIMONY TO ANSWERED PRAYER

Background: This psalm may be related to the time in David's life when he was fleeing from Saul. Some also believe that this psalm was used as a personal testimony given in public worship.

Theme: Thanksgiving for deliverance from trouble

Reader insights: An individual lament. Many scholars believe there are two psalms here. The first part of the psalm is a thanksgiving, and the second is a lament. The two are connected by a transitional verse (v. 12). The second half of the psalm (vv. 13–17) is repeated as Psalm 70.

PSALM SUMMARY

A testimony to answered prayer (40:1–12). The psalmist "waited patiently" for the Lord, not with defeated resignation but in expectant hope. It appears that there was no immediate answer, but God did eventually come to the psalmist's rescue. He "heard my cry" (v. 1).

The Lord draws the psalmist up from the pit. He was sinking down into the miry clay of death, like a person helpless in quicksand. Because of its miry bottom, there was nowhere to gain a firm footing. Note the contrast: the Lord lifted him up. He "set my feet on a rock," making him secure (v. 2). The rock is God Himself (Ps. 31:2).

Jeremiah was placed in the mud and mire of a literal pit (see Jer. 38), but there is no reason to think of the words *pit*, *mud*, and *mire* as anything more than metaphors in Psalm 40.

The results of the psalmist's deliverance are two-fold: (1) God gives him "a new song" of praise; and (2) many will see what God did for him and put their trust in the Lord (v. 3).

The beatitude in verse 4 is much like Psalm 1:1–3. Happy is the person who trusts in the Lord. He does not go astray after false gods (literally "lies"). The psalmist celebrates God's mighty acts on his behalf (v. 5). He concludes that they were incomparable and innumerable. Counting one's blessings can be a helpful spiritual exercise.

The psalmist expresses his gratitude by giving himself to the Lord in self-dedication. He knows the Lord would rather have his obedience than a thank offering. God delights more in an ethical lifestyle than in ritual correctness. This was the message of the great prophets (Amos 4:4–5; Hos. 6:6; Jer. 7:2–23). "I desire to do your will . . . your law is within my heart" (v. 8). He told the good news of his deliverance, giving his testimony to the congregation (v. 9).

"I waited patiently"

This is a very intensive expression in the Hebrew language. Literally, it reads, "Expecting, I expected."

79

In verse 10 we have a listing of the attributes of the Lord: saving power, faithfulness, steadfast love. God is altogether trustworthy. This is what called forth the psalmist's praise.

At verse 12 the psalm makes a transition from thanksgiving to lament. The psalmist is suffering from serious illness and distress. He cannot see his way out of his problem, and he feels overwhelmed by evil and trouble.

A prayer for future deliverance (40:13–17). The psalmist cries out for deliverance from his enemies (vv. 13–14). Their mockery causes him to pray for their punishment (v. 15). He feels his own weakness but is equally aware of God's power: "The Lord be exalted!" (v. 16). Therefore, he can trust God to take care of him.

See Psalm 70 for a repetition of this part of the psalm. The blending of two poems in Psalm 40 is appropriate, for joy and suffering are often two sides of the same coin.

■ *The psalmist prays for deliverance from his*
■ *enemies and then trusts God to care for him.*

GUIDING QUESTIONS

What is the psalmist's predicament? What does God do for him?

PSALM 41: BLESSED ARE THE MERCIFUL

Theme: A prayer for one suffering from sickness
Reader insights: An individual lament. Verses 1–3 are very similar to Jesus' beatitude in which He taught that those who show mercy also receive mercy (Matt. 5:7).

PSALM SUMMARY

The rewards of the compassionate (41:1–4). This section sounds a positive note. "Blessed is he who has regard for the weak!" (v. 1). We find a similar beatitude in James 1:27.

The psalmist mentions seven blessings He gives to those who show mercy. He delivers them, protects them, keeps them alive, sustains them, blesses them in the land, does not allow enemies to get the best of them, and restores them from all sickness.

Background: Psalm 1 celebrates the happiness of a righteous person. Psalm 32 celebrates the blessedness of a forgiven sinner. And Psalm 41 celebrates the happiness of the compassionate.

A lament against friend and enemy (41:5–10). The psalmist recounts his past distress. He had prayed for healing, acknowledging his sins against God (v. 4). His enemies are malicious. They anxiously await his death, like vultures (v. 5).

One of the psalmist's enemies pays him a visit. What appears to be an act of mercy is actually an effort to see how ill he really is and report it to everyone else (v. 6). His enemies start a whisper campaign against him. They speculate as to what terrible sin on his part had brought on his serious sickness. They "imagine the worst" (v. 7). How true to human nature!

Finally, the psalmist's enemies conclude that he has "a vile disease"—some terminal disease or

The cruelest blow of all occurs when the psalmist's best friend joins the ranks of his enemies. The two had shared mutual trust and common meals together, but this "bosom friend" turns against him (v. 9). Jesus quoted the last half of this verse, referring to the treachery of Judas's betrayal (John 13:18).

perhaps a curse. They are convinced that he will never recover (v. 8).

In verse 10 we have a strange prayer. The psalmist asks God to be gracious and heal him in order that he might pay back his enemies! His healing will prove them wrong. Jesus taught that we should not try to take revenge on our enemies. Vengeance belongs to God alone (Rom. 12:19). The prayer is, of course, pre-Christian, but it is also very human. It is out of keeping with the psalmist's own attitude in verses 1–3.

Healing proves to be vindication (41:11–12). God's healing the psalmist fully shows that God is pleased with his integrity. It stops the tongues of his enemies and shows that his relationship with God, broken by his sin (v. 4), had been restored.

Benediction (41:13). Verse 13 is a benediction to Book One of the Psalms. It concludes with a double "Amen" to be repeated by the congregation in worship.

■ *God heals the psalmist, and this stops the*
■ *tongues of his enemies. His relationship with*
■ *God, broken by his sin, has now been*
■ *restored.*

GUIDING QUESTION

What blessings does God give to those who show mercy?

PSALMS 42–43: HOMESICK FOR GOD

Theme: Dealing with spiritual depression

Reader insights: An individual lament. The two psalms taken together have three sections, each of which concludes with a refrain (42:5, 11; 43:5). The psalmist gives vivid expression to his longing for God and the experience of public worship.

PSALM SUMMARY

A thirst for God (42:1–5). As the deer thirsts for flowing streams in times of drought, so the psalmist longs for the living God, who never fails to satisfy (vv. 1–2). Overwhelmed by his depression and surrounded by scoffers, the psalmist thirsts for the comfort of God's presence. As the stream quenches the deer's thirst, so God's steadfast love brings joy and praise to the psalmist's lips.

The psalmist is so homesick for God that he loses all appetite—tears are his only food. Scoffers taunt him, asking, "Where is your God?" (v. 3). This statement brings to mind the sarcasm and insults hurled at Jesus on the cross (Matt. 27:43).

The psalmist recalls happier days when he had been in the pilgrim's procession going up to the house of God for worship. Those were times of joy and thanksgiving (v. 4).

The psalmist talks with himself in an effort to find encouragement and overcome depression. He calls on himself to hope and wait for God.

Feeling overwhelmed (42:6–11). The author finds himself in the north, away from Jerusalem. The

Background: While these two psalms are separate, they make up a single poem. The poet was a person of deep faith who was living in exile at the headwaters of the Jordan River near Mount Hermon, north of the Holy Land. While he could pray to the Lord, he sincerely missed the opportunities for worship at the Temple in Jerusalem.

sound of the waterfalls or cataracts is like thunder. He thinks of the depths of the sea and feels overwhelmed by his depression (v. 7). In the dark night of his soul, the Lord gives him a night song (v. 8).

God is still his rock—his source of strength and security. Even so, he feels deserted at times (v. 9). His enemies are still taunting his faith (vv. 3, 10). The refrain occurs a second time (v. 11).

Praying for vindication (43:1–5). The psalmist asks God to defend him and deliver him from the ungodly (v. 1). The silence and absence of God are at times unbearable for him (v. 2). He prays for God to send His light and truth, benevolent messengers, who will bring him to the "altar of God" again with great joy (v. 4). This time the refrain emphasizes hope and becomes a shout of triumph (v. 5).

- *The psalmist finds the cure for his depres-*
- *sion. He asks God to defend him and deliver*
- *him from the ungodly. He then places his*
- *hope in the Lord.*

GUIDING QUESTION

The psalm provides us with the cure for spiritual depression. What are its steps?

PSALM 44: WHERE ON EARTH IS GOD?

Theme: A lament after a defeat in battle
Reader insight: A community lament.

PSALM SUMMARY

Praying for vindication (44:1–5). What happens to faith in a time of national military defeat? The psalmist knew his history and set the present trouble in perspective. Their fathers had related God's mighty acts on behalf of His people in earlier times. The book of Joshua records the events cited here. He drove the Canaanites out and established Israel in the land. Neither their swords nor their might won the victories; God did it on behalf of His people.

Israel's present trust in God (44:4–8). Israel still acknowledged God as their king, giving Him the glory for their triumphs. Their faith was not simply in their arms. Because of God's blessings in the past, Israel was confident they could trust Him for the present and the future. Then came the bombshell!

When faith and fact do not agree (44:9–22). Despite Israel's faith, they were defeated. God had not marched with their armies, giving them victory (v. 9). He had not performed mighty acts on their behalf. Some Israelites were slaughtered like sheep, and others were sold into slavery for a pittance (vv. 11–12).

The hardest pill to swallow was the ridicule and scorn of their enemies. The entire nation was a laughingstock held up to derision (vv. 13–16). All this had happened to the Israelites even though they had been faithful to God (vv.

Background: The context in which the psalm was used in worship may be reflected in 2 Chronicles 20:1–19. The king would have read it in a time of national crisis or calamity. Israel had trusted in God, yet they met with disaster. Their armies were defeated, their citizens were sold into slavery, and their cities were razed. The national disgrace and shame were unbearable.

Their lament (vv. 20–22). Note the lament in verse 22. Paul quotes it in Romans 8:36 to show that believers often face persecution and death for their faith. Israel's theological problem was that they believed God blessed in proportion to their obedience and cursed in proportion to their disobedience. Contrast that view with the experience of Job and with Isaiah 53.

17–18). Their cities were left desolate, inhabited only by jackals (v. 19).

They cry for help (44:23–26). The psalmist wonders where God is. He concludes that He must be asleep, and prays to awaken Him! This may seem strange to modern Christians (see Ps. 121:4). The love of God revealed in Christ was veiled to the psalmist; still, he trusts in God (v. 26).

It is interesting to note that Israel's painful and crushing experience did not cause disbelief in God. What troubled them the most was their inability to understand God's ways.

N

- Despite Israel's genuine faith, they were
- defeated. They became the ridicule and scorn
- of their enemies. Their view of God was
- faulty. They believed He blessed them in pro-
- portion to their obedience and cursed in pro-
- portion to their disobedience.

GUIDING QUESTION
Israel's military defeat must have been devastating to the nation, especially since they had been obedient to God. What was their problem?

PSALM 45: A ROYAL WEDDING

Background: This psalm celebrates a royal wedding. It is a joyous tribute to the king and his bride on a festive occasion. A royal wedding was an event of national importance. It would ensure the continuation of the dynasty (v. 16). It is not possible to identify the original occasion of the psalm's use.

Theme: A royal marriage song

Reader insights: A royal wedding song. Later Jewish interpretation applied this royal psalm to the king as the Messiah and the bride as Israel. In the New Testament, we see that Christ is the King and the church is His bride.

PSALM SUMMARY

To the king (45:1–9). After a short introduction, the psalmist speaks in first person and addresses the king in a song of praise. The psalmist is excited about his subject. His tongue is as ready as the pen of a fast stenographer (v. 1). His praise of the king and his bride is filled with extravagant superlatives.

His character (v. 2). He declares that the king is handsome and that his words are winsome. The king also enjoys the blessings of God.

His military prowess (vv. 3–5). Next, the psalmist celebrates the king's prowess as a warrior. He wields a mighty sword, rides forth in victory, defends truth and the right, and fires sharp arrows, putting dread into his foes.

His rule (vv. 6–7). The king will be an ethical ruler, loving justice, and hating wrong. The promise in verse 6 is that his divinely established throne will last forever (a common but vain promise if applied to anyone less than the Messiah). The king represents God as His adopted Son (see Ps. 2:7).

His wedding (vv. 8–9). The king's wedding day is a time of great joy. God Himself anoints the king with "the oil of joy" (see Ps. 23:5). The king's regal robes are perfumed; music gladdens the occasion. Pomp is evident in the ivory-inlaid palace and the gold-bedecked queen (vv. 8–9).

Faithfulness to one's mate. (45:10–15). Addressing the bride (45:10–15), the psalmist cites an ingredient in any successful marriage—leaving one's parents to cleave to one's mate (v. 10). Her allegiance is now to belong to the king, her husband (v. 11). Neighboring states and wealthy families will bestow gifts on the new queen (v. 12).

Next, the poet describes the wedding procession. The beautifully dressed bride leads her attendants into the palace of the king "with joy and gladness" (v. 15).

The psalmist anticipates the birth of sons to the royal couple. He predicts that they would be worthy princes, bringing honor to their father and the praise of the populace. The ultimate blessing of the marriage is that of children.

This poem of celebration shows clearly that the nation is dependent on God. God blesses the king (v. 2), establishes his throne (v. 6), chooses the king (v. 7), and gives him sons to ensure the future of the kingdom (v. 16).

■ *The psalmist pictures a bright future in*
■ *which God blesses the king. The ultimate*
■ *blessing of the marriage is that of children.*

GUIDING QUESTIONS

What is the background for this psalm? How is this psalm interpreted in light of the New Testament?

Psalm 46: The City of God

Theme: Confidence in God's power and ultimate victory

Reader insights: A hymn. Here is one of the most influential psalms in the history of the church. It is a hymn in praise of the presence of God. There are two stanzas with a refrain: "The LORD Almighty is with us; the God of Jacob is our fortress" (vv. 7, 11). Although the psalm never uses the word *faith*, its theme is faith in the sovereign power and ultimate victory of God. Psalm 46 also inspired Martin Luther's great Reformation hymn, "A Mighty Fortress Is Our God."

PSALM SUMMARY

God, our refuge (46:1–3). These verses refer to God's activity in nature, specifically His creation. They constitute a backward glance. At creation God brought order out of chaos. He continues to exert control over nature. These are crashing sentences, illuminated with flashes of lightning. This brings to mind Jesus' stilling the storm on the Sea of Galilee, saying, "Quiet! Be still!" (Mark 4:39).

The teaching of this passage is that though the world about us is disturbed, the faithful need not be frightened. Faith survives because God is our help and refuge. Believers need have no ultimate fear, for they are secure. Faith remains, as God remains, when all else fails (Rom. 8:31–39).

God, our help (46:4–7). He is not only our Creator but also our sustainer. These verses have a present reference. The city of God was Jerusalem, which had no river like other capitals. Babylon

Background: The occasion that inspired this and the following two psalms was likely the invasion of land by the army of Sennacherib during the reign of King Hezekiah of Judah. We can see similarities between the language of this psalm and that of Isaiah, who lived through that crisis and wrote about it.

"Ever-present help in trouble"

The word translated *ever-present* is the Hebrew word that means "exceedingly."

was built on the Euphrates, Egypt alongside the Nile, and Rome on the Tiber. The stream that refreshes Jerusalem is the presence of the living God (see Rev. 21:1-5*a*; 22:1-5 for a description of the new Jerusalem).

God, our hope (46:8-11). This third stanza of the psalm has a future stance; it looks ahead. A time is coming when wars will cease and the peace of God will reign. God will be exalted: "Be still, and know that I am God." This statement is not intended to encourage us to a contemplative life; rather, it means to desist from warlike activities designed to win supremacy.

God has all power, and His divine purpose cannot suffer ultimate defeat. He will have the last word, and His kingdom will come. His will shall be done on earth as it is in heaven. What a source of encouragement for the believer!

Again, note the refrain (v. 11). "The Lord of hosts" (KJV) is a reference to His heavenly armies, the angels. The phrase reminds us of His unseen might that fights evil on our behalf.

"The God of Jacob" is an historical reference. Our faith is not simply other worldly. It is anchored in history here on earth. God has acted on our behalf. His intervention reveals His will for us. We see it in such events as His choice of Abraham, the deliverance of the Israelites in the Exodus, and the sending of his Son, Jesus Christ. Our faith has to do with both here and hereafter. One day the kingdoms of this world shall become the kingdom of our Lord and of His Christ.

- *A time is coming when wars will cease and*
- *the peace of God will reign.*

GUIDING QUESTION

"There is a river whose streams make glad the city of God" (v. 4). What does the psalmist mean by this statement?

PSALM 47: KING OF ALL THE EARTH

Theme: God is king over all the earth

Reader insights: All the festivity and excitement of a coronation is reflected in this psalm—and the king is God Himself! The theme of the psalm is found in verse 7: God is "the King of all the earth!" The most striking characteristic of this psalm is its universalism. That is, while God is king of Israel, he is also king of "all you nations" (v. 1). New Testament parallels to this psalm are found in the Lord's Prayer ("Your kingdom come") and Revelation 11:15 ("The kingdom of the world has become the kingdom of our Lord and of his Christ, and he will reign for ever and ever").

PSALM SUMMARY

God is king of Israel (47:1–5). Notice the ingredients of a coronation included here: the people shout and clap their hands in celebration (v. 1); there is a trumpet fanfare (v. 5); neighboring kings pay their respect. There is also a procession up to the Temple (v. 5).

Background: Scholars have suggested that this is one of six *enthronement psalms* used in Jewish worship on New Year's Day to celebrate God as king of creation and history (see also Pss. 93; 96–99).

"Jacob" in verse 4 stands for the Hebrew nation as well as for their ancestors. Clapping, shouting, and playing of trumpets were parts of the coronation ceremony.

To call God "awesome" (v. 2) means He is to be respected and revered. He defeated the people of Canaan, giving the land to Israel. Verse 5 describes the triumphant procession going up to the Temple, where God's presence is represented by the ark of the covenant in the Holy of Holies.

God is King of all people (47:6–9). In the jubilant celebration the psalmist calls for singing praise to God four times. Verses 7–8 appear to be either a choral or a congregational response: "For God is the king of all the earth . . . God reigns over the nations; God is seated on his holy throne."

"The people of the God of Abraham" in verse 9 refers to his descendants through whom "all the families of the earth shall be blessed" (Gen. 12:3, alternate translation).

God's universal kingship over all the nations of the world is declared four times in this short psalm (vv. 2, 7–9).

The psalmist's vision of God is truly worldwide. He envisioned the ultimate universal reign of the Creator—the kingdom of God. The church lives in anticipation of that time when Jesus will in fact be Lord of all.

- *God is not only King of Israel, He is King of*
- *all people. The psalmist's vision of God is*
- *truly worldwide; he declares God's universal*
- *kingship over all the nations of the world*
- *four times.*

GUIDING QUESTIONS

What New Testament parallels do we find to this psalm? What do these parallels tell us?

PSALM 48: THE CITY OF OUR GOD

Theme: God's presence in Jerusalem

Reader insights: A hymn. The theme of this psalm is an elaboration of Psalm 46:5—God's presence in Jerusalem. His presence was the city's security. The ancient Hebrews thought their Holy City could not fall. But in 587 B.C. it did.

PSALM SUMMARY

The city of the great king (48:1–3). The psalmist begins with a declaration, "Great is the LORD" (v. 1). This fact constitutes a call to praise. Jerusalem "is beautiful in its loftiness" (v. 2). He calls Jerusalem with its Temple on Mount Zion "the city of our God . . . the city of the Great King" (God). God Himself was Jerusalem's sure defense, "her fortress" (v. 3).

The city intimidates its enemies (48:4–8). Attacking kings approach Jerusalem. But as soon as they see this city is defended by God, they are "astounded." Trembling, they flee in panic and

Background: This psalm may have been sung by pilgrim worshipers marching through Jerusalem.

Geography of Jerusalem

The psalmist refers to Jerusalem's "loftiness," which is a reference to its elevation in the land. The city is over 2,500 feet above sea level. Biblical references speak of people "going up" to Jerusalem because of its elevation. Those traveling by foot would become acutely aware of this fact.

"Its elevation is remarkable; occasioned not from its being on the summit of one of the numerous hills of Judea, like most of the towns and villages, but because it is on the edge of one of the highest tablelands of the country" (*The Psalms* [New York: Soncino Press, 1974], 149).

East Wind

The psalmist refers to the east wind in speaking of the defeat and destruction of the enemy. The east wind, or scirroco, was a hot, sweltering wind that would suddenly sweep in and dry out vegetation and threaten life in general. Here it is viewed as a symbol of destructive power. Ironically, it was the east wind that parted the Red Sea and saved the Israelites from the Egyptians.

gasp with anguish like a woman in childbirth (v. 6). They are broken up and demolished like mighty merchant ships from Spain in the grip of a storm from the east (v. 7). God has both established and defended Jerusalem in the past. And God's people are confident of His continuing protection in the future.

Touring the city with praise and joy (48:9–14). In verses 10–12, the worshipers address God directly. They focus on His covenantal characteristics: lovingkindness, righteousness, judgments.

Pilgrims are invited to tour Jerusalem, taking note of its towers, ramparts, and citadels (vv. 12–13). They are admonished to tell unborn generations that God is the city's God and sure defense "even to the end" (v. 14). The procession is designed to imprint upon the hearts of the worshipers a reality of the living God. The Jew's reverence for the Holy City is similar to that which Christians give to Christ.

■ *Worshipers tour the city with praise and joy.*
■ *They acknowledge God's character in their*
■ *praise of Him, and they are admonished to*
■ *tell unborn generations that He is the God of*
■ *Jerusalem.*

GUIDING QUESTION

Although Jerusalem was a formidable, natural fortress, what was its true defense?

Psalm 49: What Money Cannot Buy

Background: This psalm is not a hymn or a prayer addressed to God, but rather a proverb from a wise teacher addressed to people.

Theme: The inadequacy of riches and the inevitability of death
Reader insight: A wisdom song.

PSALM SUMMARY

Now hear this! (49:1–4). The wisdom teacher's introduction is universal in its appeal. It captures the attention of rich and poor alike. The wise teacher's proverb promises to solve a riddle (a tough problem) that was of interest to all mankind.

■ *Capturing the attention of rich and poor*
■ *alike, the wise teacher's proverb promises to*
■ *solve a riddle of universal interest.*

What money cannot buy (49:5–12). Woe to those who trust in their wealth and boast about their riches. Money cannot postpone death or buy immortality (vv. 7, 9). Death is impartial and indiscriminate, for it takes the wealthy and the poor alike. Those who own vast lands ultimately occupy no more than a grave space.

Despite all mankind's pride and pomp, his lot is the same as that of the animals—to die. It is a chilling refrain which emphasizes the stark reality of death. We find the psalm's refrain in verses 12 and 20.

The theme of this psalm was later expanded in the teachings of Jesus in His parables of the rich fool (Luke 12:16–21) and Lazarus and the rich man (Luke 16:19–31). It was exemplified in the text from Jesus. A person's life does not consist in the abundance of possessions (Luke 12:15). The psalm is a warning about the limitations of wealth.

■ *Wealth and riches offer no advantages in*
■ *death. Death is impartial, taking the wise*
■ *and foolish as well as the rich and poor.*

Death is their shepherd (49:13–14). The wise teacher continues his theme. The rich are so pleased with themselves. Perhaps they consider themselves self-made men. With biting irony the writer reminds them that death is their shepherd and the grave will be their sheepfold. Sheol (the Pit) will be their home.

This is remarkable faith on the part of the psalmist. The psalmist is confident that God would one day do for him what riches could not—ransom his soul from death. "No man can redeem the life of another or give to God a ransom for him" (v. 7). Jesus gave his life as "a ransom for many" (Mark 10:45).

A glimpse of glory (49:15). This verse shines like a diamond on black velvet! The dark background of the psalm makes it all the brighter. Old Testament believers had no clear view of life after death. Job longed for it (Job 19:25–27), but with no certain revelation of its reality.

We cannot take it with us (49:16–20). Having sounded this high hope, the psalmist returns to his theme. He admonishes his readers: "Do not be overawed when a man grows rich" (v. 16). There is no need to envy or fear the rich (v. 16). When they die they have no pockets in their shrouds. They will "take nothing" with them (v. 17). No matter how happy we are here on earth, death awaits us all (vv. 18–19). The refrain occurs a second time (v. 20).

■ *There is no need to envy or fear the rich.*
■ *Their privileged position in life will not give*
■ *them the same in death. Death, it has been*
■ *said, is the "great equalizer."*

GUIDING QUESTIONS

Describe the wise teacher's confidence in God. How far-reaching is it?

PSALM 50: THE LORD, OUR JUDGE

Theme: The kingship of God

Reader insights: A hymn. This psalm rebukes our "playing church" and calls for heartfelt worship. It is much like the message of the eighth-century B.C. Hebrew prophets.

PSALM SUMMARY

The judge of all the earth (50:1–6). God summons the world to judgment, both His chosen people, Israel, and the wicked. He is both plaintiff and judge in the case (cp. Isa. 41; 43).

"The Mighty One," the Creator, summons all the earth "from the rising of the sun to the place where it sets" before the bar of judgment (v. 1). He sits in judgment "from Zion," Jerusalem. His appearance is similar to that at Mount Sinai (Exod. 19). Our God comes in a storm, laced with lightning (v. 3). He calls on heaven and earth to witness the trial of his saints—"my consecrated ones" (v. 5). "God himself is judge" (v. 6).

The gift without the giver (50:7–15). God is not displeased that His people are bringing their sacrifices to Him. But they misunderstood the meaning behind their gifts. They assumed that God needed their sacrifice. "Do I eat the flesh of bulls, or drink the blood of goats?" (v. 13). Everything belongs to God, "the cattle on a thousand hills" (v. 10).

The motive behind our worship is not God's need—but ours! Therefore, the sacrifice God really wants is our heartfelt worship and thanksgiving (v. 14) and our fellowship with Him in prayer (v. 15). God's ownership of all is the basis of stewardship. He doesn't need our money, but we need to learn the joy of giving. It is a cure for our selfishness.

Testimony against the hypocrites (50:16–21). The wicked can recite the Ten Commandments by heart; yet they are not ethical in their daily lives (v. 16). They despise discipline (v. 17), associate with thieves and adulterers, and slander their own brothers (vv. 18–20). This passage is similar to Hosea 4:12 and Romans 2:17–24. Their religion is merely an external tradition—not a matter of the heart. God the Judge will deliver the indictment of hypocrisy to the wicked. They must answer to Him.

Warning and promise (50:22–23). A terrifying judgment awaits those who talk the talk but whose hearts are not in it. But those who walk in God's ways will know His salvation and blessing (vv. 22–23).

N

■ *Religion is merely an external tradition to*
■ *the wicked. They simply go through the*
■ *motions because their religion is not a matter*
■ *of the heart. God's people are challenged to*
■ *live ethically and in gratitude for His divine*
■ *grace. By doing so, they show the fruits of*
■ *their salvation and bring honor to God.*

GUIDING QUESTION

What is the psalmist's warning to those who engage a superficial religion and "play church"?

CHRIST IN THE PSALMS

One of the most controversial questions facing interpreters of the book of Psalms is how to understand the many references to the "king" or "anointed one" (Hebrew *Messiah*). Do these references speak of a human king of ancient Israel or point ahead to Jesus as the ideal King and Messiah?

The biblical writers wrote of real-life persons and situations. The king played a most prominent role in ancient Israel's national life. More than sixty references in the Psalms highlight the king's prestige. The original readers of the Psalms naturally understood that these references spoke of the human king, whose role was so very important in their day-to-day existence. Because the basic meaning of any text is what the author intended the original audience to understand, "king" in the Psalms refers primarily to a human king of ancient Israel.

It may be possible for references to the "king" or "anointed one" to speak of both a human king and point ahead to Jesus as the ideal One.

The only clear passage that describes a human king in its Old Testament context who is seen as the ideal messianic King in a subsequent text is Psalm 2 (Heb. 1:5 treats this psalm as explicitly messianic). Thus, the human king in Psalm 2 functioned as a type, that is, one who had significance in his own historical setting but who also served as a divinely ordained foreshadowing of someone in later biblical revelation.

Generally speaking, references to the king in Psalms speak of the human king in the biblical writer's time. Occasionally, reference to the king was originally understood as a human king but later applied to the ideal Messiah. In one psalm (Ps. 110) the king can mean none other than the ideal messianic King of kings.

The superscription of Psalm 110 portrays it as Davidic. Surprisingly, the first verse speaks of David's successor as his lord. In ancient Israel this was inconceivable. David was the greatest king, the standard by which his successors were measured. Early in Israel's history this passage was understood as a prophecy of the coming Messiah. Jesus interpreted Psalm 110:1 in this way in a dispute with the Pharisees (Matt. 22:41–55; Mark 12:35–37; Luke 20:41–44). Jesus' riddle—if "David himself calls him 'Lord,' how then can he be his son?"—captures the mystery of the incarnation. Jesus is the Son of David but also more than David's son (Rom. 1:3–4).

(Taken from *Holman Bible Handbook*, p. 340.)

TYPES OF OLD TESTAMENT LITERATURE

It helps to understand the Old Testament if we know what type of literature we are reading in any particular passage. For example, the meaning of Amos 5:2 is clearer when we know it is a funeral song. Or Psalm 17 loses its seeming self-righteousness when we know it is the lament of one falsely accused of a crime.

Since the turn of the century, biblical scholars have classified and named various types of Old Testament literature. By comparing them with similar forms found in other ancient Near Eastern literature, scholars have delineated their typical traits and attempted to place them in their original situations in Israel's life. This branch of biblical science is called *form criticism*.

Form criticism says nothing about the historical basis of an Old Testament passage. The names of the forms refer to the literary structures in the stories. There are no complete myths (timeless stories of the gods and their relationships) in the Old Testament. The God of the Bible is one God, who acts in history. Occasionally some of the language of ancient Near Eastern myths is borrowed, for example, from the Mesopotamian chaos dragon myth (Ps. 74:13–14; Isa. 51:9). In such cases that language is always used in a historical context.

Most of the Old Testament's forms were first shaped and handed down orally before being written down (although there are some exceptions; for example, the biographical portions of Jeremiah). Typical structures made the forms easy to remember and pass on by word of mouth. By knowing the typical structure of a form, we are able to see how any biblical author has changed the form and thus given it a particular emphasis. For example, Jeremiah 15:15–18 has the form of an individual lament. Laments are usually followed by an expression of trust and hope (as in Jer. 20:7–13). But Jeremiah 15:18 is followed by a challenge from God, thus emphasizing 15:19–21.

The various types of Old Testament literature found are almost too many to list. Among prose types are speeches (2 Kings 18:28–35), sermons (Jer. 7:1–15), prayers (1 Kings 8:23–53), letters (1 Kings 21:8–10), and lists. Other prose forms include rules governing worship and sacrifice (Lev. 1–7), short stories (Ruth and the Joseph story), fables (Judg. 9:8–15), and autobiographies (Neh. 1–7).

Other representatives of prose forms are accounts of dreams and visions (Gen. 37:5–10), proverbs (1 Sam. 10:12), riddles (Judg. 14:18), wisdom sayings (Proverbs), and allegories (Ezek. 17:22–24). Second Samuel 6–20 and 1 Kings 1–2 are generally acknowledged to be eyewitness histories written by someone in David's court.

There are several collections of laws. The most important are the Decalogue or Ten Commandments (Exod. 20:1–17; Deut. 5:6–21), the Book of the Covenant (Exod. 20:22–23:33), the Holiness Code (Lev. 17–26), and the book of Deuteronomy, which is shaped in the form of sermons.

Among poetic types are songs of all kinds: work songs (Num. 21:17–18), love songs (Song of Songs), mocking songs (Isa. 14:4–21), victory songs (Exod. 15:21), funeral songs (Lamentations). Worship songs include the forms found in the Psalter: hymns of praise (Ps. 96), thanksgivings (Ps. 116), songs of Zion (Ps. 48), royal psalms (Pss. 2; 110), both individual (Ps. 22) and communal (Ps. 44) laments, processional hymns (Ps. 15), songs of trust (Ps. 27), enthronement hymns (Ps. 72), and wisdom psalms (Ps. 49).

The two most frequent types found in the Psalter are the hymn and the individual lament. These represent the two poles of Israel's worship, praise and lament. The hymn structure is found throughout the Bible. It opens with a call to praise or to bless God (Ps. 98:1a). This is followed by the transitional word *for* and a sentence giving the reason for the praise (Ps. 98:1b). Or it is followed by sentences beginning with "who" that describe God's person or activity (cp. Ps. 103:3–5). Then follows the hymn body, giving a further description of God (Ps. 98:1c–3). Sometimes there is a conclusion (Ps. 104:34–35); sometimes the structure of the hymn is just repeated (Ps. 98:4–9). This typical hymn structure may be seen still in use in the New Testament (for example, Luke 1:46–55). The purpose of a hymn is always to praise God.

The lament also has a typical form. It opens with an invocation of God (Ps. 22:1–5) followed by a description of the sufferer's situation (Ps. 22:6–8, 14–18). There is then petition to God for all (Ps. 22:11, 19–21). A lament usually closes with the expression of certainty that God has heard the prayer and will save (Ps. 22:22–31). That is, lament turns into praise.

In the prophetic literature we find oracles of judgment on both individuals (Amos 7:14–17) and nations (Isa. 8:6–8), oracles of salvation (Jer. 35:18–19), and woe oracles (Isa. 5:8–10, often put in a series as in Isa. 5:11–25). Other prophetic forms include legal procedures (Isa. 1:18–20) and prophetic Torahs (Isa. 1:10–17).

The basic structure of the prophetic oracle of judgment is as follows: Introduction (Amos 4:1a, b), a description of Israel's sinful situation (Amos 4:1c, d), the messenger formula that indicates that the oracle comes from God (Amos 4:2a), and the announcement of God's coming action (Amos 4:2b–3). This form was used until the time of Ezekiel, although with variations.

The Old Testament is a marvel of literary variety and form.

(Taken from *Holman Bible Handbook*, pp. 324–25.)

VENGEANCE AND VINDICATION

Sensitive readers of the Psalms have long been troubled by the harsh expression of vengeance uttered by psalmists, often attributed to David himself. Take for example these statements:

• "Break the arm of the wicked and evil man: call him to account for his wickedness" (Ps. 10:15);

• "Let the wicked be put to shame and lie silent in the grave" (Ps. 31:17); and

• "The righteous will be glad when they are avenged, when they bathe their feet in the blood of the wicked" (Ps. 58:6–10).

Such unloving statements raise serious ethical questions about the vindictive spirit reflected in these statements. Other prominent curses are found in Psalms 3:7; 5:10; 28:4; 35; 40:14–15; 55; 69; 79; 109; 137; 139.19–22; 140:9 10. Attempts to explain such fierce expressions fall into several categories.

First, some think that these curses only reflect the humanity of the author expressing his deepest desires for vindication when wronged by the wicked.

Thus, he was reflecting a lower standard of morality than that found in the New Testament. This explanation does not adequately account for the fact that the verses in which these curses occur are inspired by the very God who taught the virtue of turning the other cheek.

We must also recognize that 1 Samuel portrays David in a very different light. Although provoked almost beyond imagination, David did not respond vengefully but by tolerance and patience. The occasions on which David refused to kill his mortal enemy Saul provide elo-quent testimony to this. Furthermore, Leviticus 19:18 forbids any attempt to exact vengeance against personal enemies, arguing against interpreting these curses as personal vendettas.

Second, another explanation sees the curses as only predictions of the enemy's ruin rather than as expressions of the psalmist's desire that the enemy meet an unhappy end. But Psalm 59 is clearly a prayer to God in which the psalmist asks God to wreak havoc on his enemies.

A plausible understanding of these difficult sayings must take account of the significant role enemies play in the book of Psalms. Their pres-ence goes far beyond the relatively limited number of psalms that curse the psalmist's enemies. The psalmists were often kings or rep-resented the king in some official capacity. God mandated Israel's king to rule over God's covenant people in order to safeguard them and all God had promised to do through them.

Thus, any threat to God's people was also a threat to the very promise of God. In this unique situation, to oppose the God-anointed king was to oppose God Himself. So the king/psalmist prayed that God would judge those evildoers who intended to hinder the work of God, desiring that God and His work on earth would be vindicated.

Because of the unique position held by the king as God's anointed, he represented God's will in a measure unlike that of anyone today. For this reason believers today must not pray curses, for they are not in a position like that of the king/psalmist in ancient Israel.

(Taken from *Holman Bible Handbook*, p. 335.)

The following list is a collection of the sources used for this volume. All are from Broadman & Holman's list of published reference resources. They accommodate the reader's need for more specific information and/or for an expanded treatment of *Psalms*, vol. 1. These works will greatly aid in the reader's study, teaching, and presentation of the Psalms. The accompanying annotations can be helpful in guiding the reader to the proper resources.

Cate, Robert L. *An Introduction to the Old Testament and Its Study*. A scholarly treatment of Old Testament issues and topics. The author deals with history and various schools of thought. He presents his material in such a way that the reader can grasp the content of the Old Testament and come to view it as a book of faith.

Holman Bible Dictionary. An exhaustive, alphabetically arranged resource of Bible-related subjects. An excellent tool of definitions and other information on the people, places, things, and events of the Bible.

Holman Bible Handbook, pp. 323-50. A comprehensive treatment that offers outlines, commentary on key themes and sections, and full-color photos, illustrations, charts, and maps. Provides an accent on the broader theological teachings.

Holman Book of Biblical Charts, Maps, and Reconstructions. A colorful, visual collection of charts, maps, and reconstructions, These well-designed tools are invaluable to the study of the Bible.

McEachern, Alton H. *Psalms* (Layman's Bible Book Commentary, vol. 8). A popular-level treatment of the Psalms. This easy-to-use volume provides a relevant and practical perspective for the reader. *Shepherd's Notes—Psalms 1–50* has drawn heavily on many of the outlines from Dr. McEachern's volume.

McQuay, Earl P. *Keys to Interpreting the Bible.* This work provides a fine introduction to the study of the Bible that is invaluable for home Bible studies, lay members of a local church, or students.

SHEPHERD'S NOTES

_____

_____

_____

_____

_____

_____

_____

_____

_____

_____

_____

_____

_____

_____

_____

_____

_____

SHEPHERD'S NOTES